She's A Doll

She's A Doll: The Vision, The Mission
by Brenda B. Mosely

Published in the United States by:
Brenda B Mosely African American Doll Collection, Inc.
37 Stature Drive
Newark, Delaware 19713

Produced in the United States of America.
Main entry under title:
She's A Doll: The Vision, The Mission

Brenda B Mosely African American Doll Collection Book
ISBN: 9780615760681

Website: http://www.bmoselydolls.org

Photographs, book design, and editing by
eTechPublish, Incorporated

Table of Contents

Preface

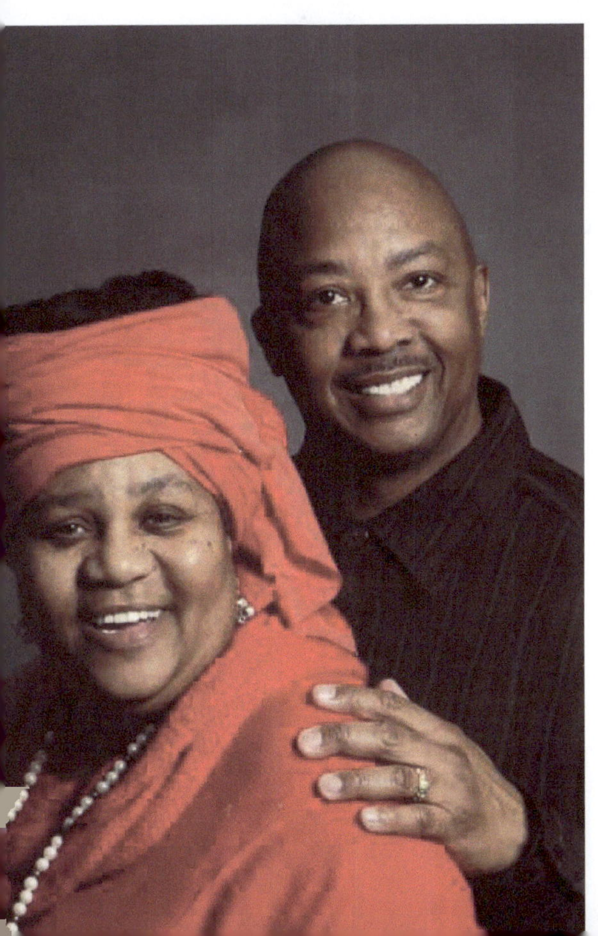

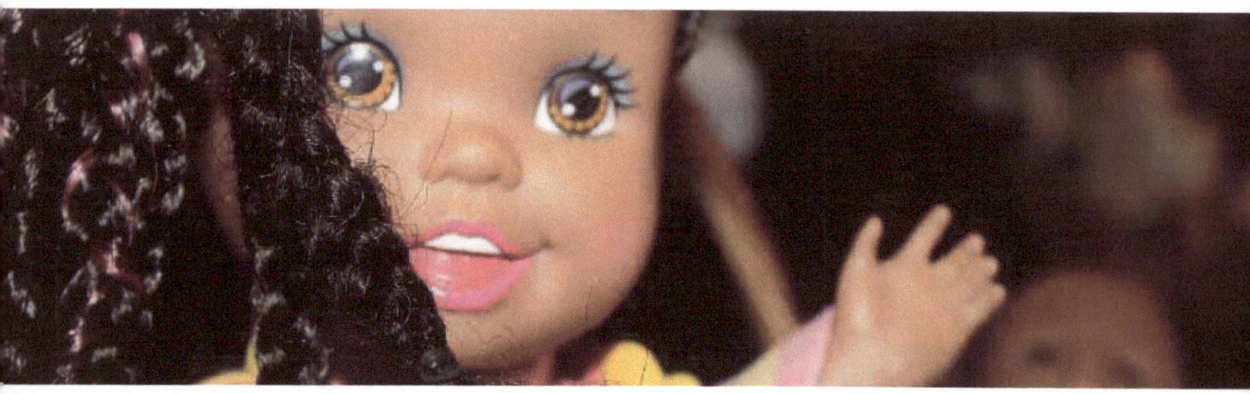

Of course, no book is ever written without the help of others. Along the way to completing any manuscript, every author encounters friends and adversaries who motivate or discourage him/her, who inspire or deflate him/her. Nevertheless, it is a pleasure to thank all of those who helped me in this venture.

This book is about the birth and maturation of an African American doll collection. The Mosely African American Doll Collection is currently located in Newark, Delaware at the home of Eric & Brenda Brown Mosely. We have 3,000 plus dolls in this collection. Our prayer is that one day the Lord will bless us with a building with ample parking space for buses. We would also like the museum to be located in the city of Wilmington, Delaware.

Our African American doll collection is based on pride, passion and love. We would be delighted and proud to share the wonderful art, books, decor, dolls, literature, and movies with the public by putting them in a museum for everyone to see.

Special Dedication

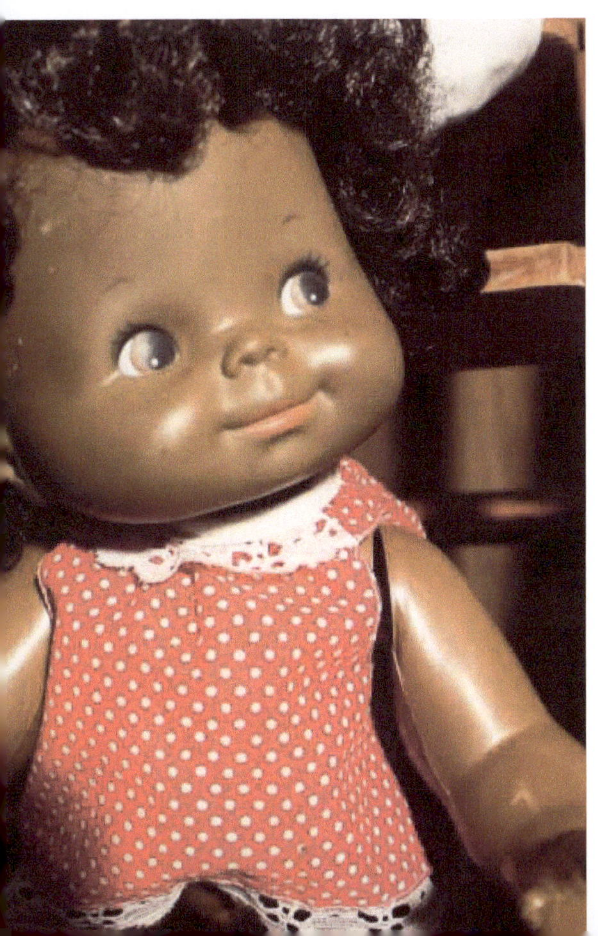

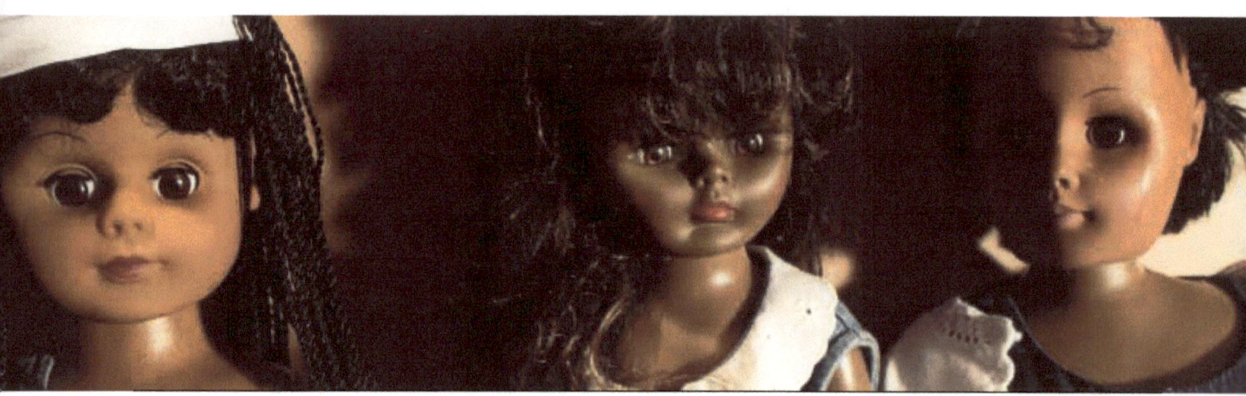

The Mosely African American Doll Collection project required an extraordinary amount of energy, enthusiasm, and hard work—reading literally hundreds of books, visiting many libraries, and discussions, insights, and advice from family and friends. I thank each and everyone.

In particular, I owe an enormous debt of gratitude to my partner for life, my husband, Eric R. Mosely, Sr., who not only gave me the space and time to put this doll collection and book together, but also encouraged his little historian wife to do so. I thank him for loving me, taking care of me, and being the most patient of all. Without him, none of this would have become a reality.

To my son, Eric R. Mosely, Jr., aka (Noon), who lifted me and encouraged me to pursue this project at the very beginning. (Only because it would all belong to him one day SMILE).

To my darling granddaughters, (vanilla and chocolate) Rosa Marie Yancey and Nyesa Gabrielle Mosely, who have promised me that they will never sell the doll collection unless it is for education or medical reasons.

And especially to all the beautiful little children who have brought their parents tears of pain, as well as tears of joy.

To my best girlfriends, in alpha order, I am blessed with loving friends like: Anita Bryant, Diane Sanford Crump, Daphne Tate Davenger, Margaret Louise Edwards, Elnore Grooms, Crystal Berrien-Hutt, Darlene Martin McBride, Colette Nicholson, Caroline Tarrent, Brenda Ward, Yvette Washington, Fay Fisher Watkins, and Betty Wilson, who offer their time and help at a moment's notice. I appreciate all of you and I Love you all unconditionally. Also, too, it is simply because you know too much HA, HA (BIG SMILE!).

To All my Sisters in age order: Dorothy Hollis Lyles, Mary Alice Brown, Delores Jean Brown, Carol Ann Brown, and Marlene Brown Marrow.

To my sister, Carol Ann Brown, who I wasn't old enough to remember too much, but somehow got a doll that someone had given her while she was in Philadelphia General Hospital. I do remember going to the hospital with my mother. The hospital was located at Uber & Dauphin Streets.

Carol died at the age of eleven in 1957 from complications resulting from a house fire. She was at our cousin's house and was trying to light the oven and her crendalin slip caught on fire. No one was in the house but her and my two younger cousins who were very close to her age and they didn't know what to do to put out the fire.

To my brother, Ralph "Shane" Brown, who taught me first to care, and then to agitate/arouse interest as to who I was as a Black girl and as an African American. It stirred up my interest in what it means to be a Black person. I learned to pursue my dreams without losing myself in the chase. Eliminate the "weeds" that hold me back. Make my life drama-free. Get past my fears so I can live and love fully. Pass the baton to future generations – especially family – by leading by example.

To My Niece, Kinshasa Marrow Townsend, a niece and a daughter to me, who always praised, admired and looked up to me. She keeps me encouraged and lets me know I am one of the Best—and always a DIVA.

To my sister-in-law, Marcia E. Mosely Francis, for editing my words and who also encouraged me to write this book.

To my goddaughters, Britney Brewington and Jessica Lowrie.

To Barbara Whiteman, my mentor and friend, who is a creative genius. She is the owner of the Philadelphia Doll Museum. Her encouragement and her suggestions and ideas have been invaluable.

For all of our ancestors, who passed down the spirit of the quest and gave me their stories as guides. And especially for me, who knows who I am and who I may be, if I choose.

To The Pioneers of African American Dolls

Ida Roberta Bell, the first African American elected into the prestigious organization of doll artists, NIADA, (National Institute of American Doll Artists.) She was inducted into the organization in 1970, as a result of the excellence in her Dr. George Washington Carver doll. She is primarily known for her portrait dolls of famous Black Americans. Professionally, she was an educator and used the dolls to impart her knowledge of Black history to her students.

Her dolls include the following: George Washington Carver; Mary McLeod Bethune; Paul Lawrence Dunbar; Harriet Tubman, Crispus Attucks, Jean Baotuste Point du Sable; W.C. Handy; Dr. Daniel Hale Williams; Frederick Douglass; Anna Murray Douglass, Frederick Douglass' wife; Elizabeth Beckley, dressmaker and confidante to Mary Todd Lincoln; Ashanti Queen Mother, queen of Ashanti(Ghana); a Black Madonna and child; Solon C. Bell, (her husband) labor leader first to establish a union among dining-car employees in the 1930's; Matthew Henson; Harold Washington, first mayor of Chicago; and Anne Davis Frierson, her maternal grandmother. Her dolls are in museums and private collections all over the country.

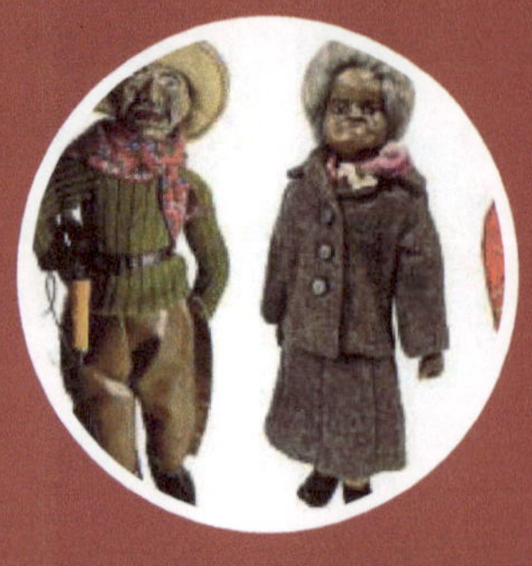

Bertabell's Dolls
Dolls made by Roberta Bell, from the left, a cowboy and Mary M. Bethune, an educator.

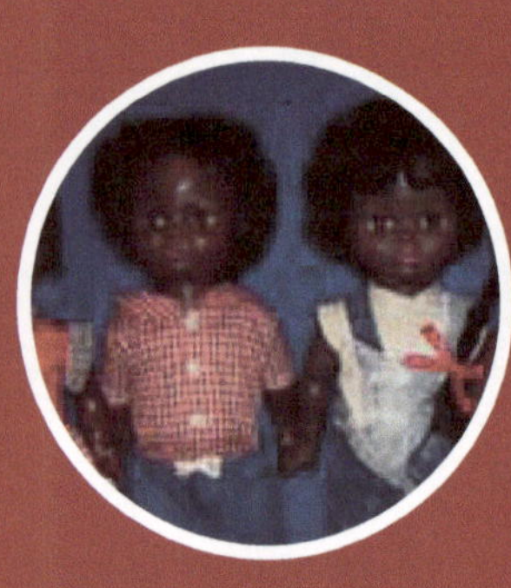

Beatrice Wright Dolls
Beatrice was the Creator, Founder and President of the first negro toy company to manufacture dolls and stuffed toys.

Bell was born in Nashville, Tennessee. At the age of eleven, she moved with her family to Kansas City, and was educated in the elementary and high schools of Topeka, Kansas, and Kansas City, Missouri.

She received a bachelor's degree from Kansas University in Lawrence, Kansas, and a master's degree from Northwestern University in Evanston, Illinois. She taught elementary school in Kansas City, Missouri and Chicago, Illinois, and retired in 1969 from the Chicago public schools.

Ida Roberta Bell came from an artist background. Her father, Robert Eugene Bell, was an artist and sculptor, as was her brother, Walter Bell. When Roberta, as she preferred to be called, was a young child, her father was upset at the fact that she had only White dolls to play with, so he removed the pink and white bisque head and hands from a doll and sculptured black ones to replace them.

Mrs. Bell later won a Black bisque-headed doll at a church raffle. The doll was ordered from a catalog by the National Negro Doll Company in Nashville, Tennessee.

Bell first began making dolls in the 1940's. She used papier-mâché, oven-hardening clay, and cloth. Wanting to perfect her craft, she took classes in mold making and painting facial features. Her famous Black Americans series was made by first modeling the head in plastilene. A mold was then made and the head and hands were poured with brown porcelain slip (liquid porcelain). The bodies were stuffed with sawdust. All costuming was done by Mrs. Bell and was thoroughly researched for detail.

Although Ida Roberta Bell had a full and rich life as a professional, her avocation was her first love. She was involved for some years with the United Federation of Doll Clubs and was founder of the Guys and Gals Funtastique Doll Club in Chicago. Presently, a doll club named in her honor is in operation in Cincinnati, Ohio.

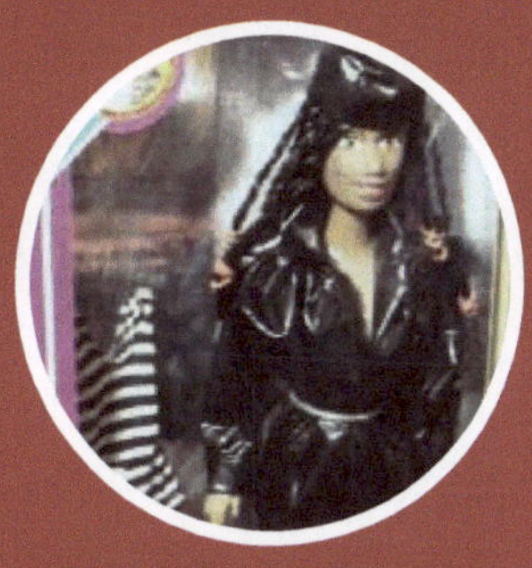

Naomi
Olmec Toys, Inc. was founded in 1985 by Yia Eason. This was the first doll created by Olmec Toys.

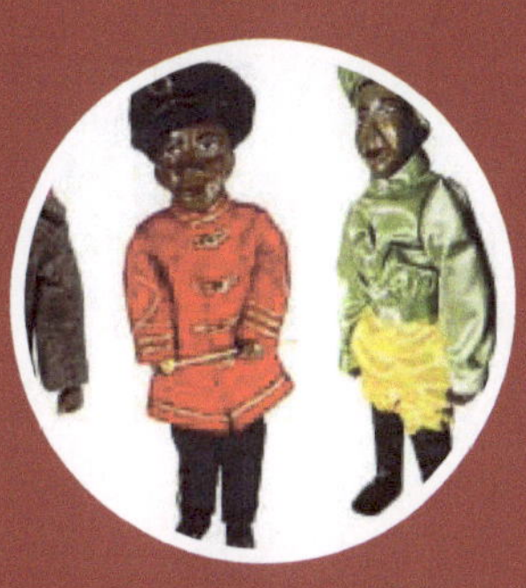

Bertabell's Dolls
Dolls made by Roberta Bell represented important people.

Beatrice Wright-Brewington was the founder and president of the first Negro toy company to manufacture dolls and stuffed toys. B. Wright's Toy Company was located at 165 North Main Street, Freeport, New York 11520.

Mrs. Wright-Brewington was born on a country farm in North Carolina and received her elementary and high school education in Faison, N.C.

She majored in elementary education and art, receiving her B.A. Degree from Shaw University, Raleigh, N.C. She attended the following schools: Hampton University in Hampton, VA; Winston Salem Teachers College, Winston, N.C.; Fayetteville State Teachers College, N.C.; Columbia University, New York, NY; Bank Street College, New York, NY.

"I LEARNED TO PURSUE MY DREAMS WITHOUT LOSING MYSELF IN THE CHASE. ELIMINATE THE "WEEDS" THAT HOLD ME BACK. MAKE MY LIFE DRAMA-FREE. GET PAST MY FEARS SO I CAN LIVE AND LOVE FULLY."

She was licensed in "Early Childhood Education", at Bank Street College. Teaching art took her to North Carolina, New York and New Jersey. In Kingston, N.C., she introduced the first art exhibit in 1946 which was then programmed for all the schools in the city, under the supervision of the School Superintendent of Lenoir County, Mr. H.H. Bullock and the principal, Mr. R.I. Flanagan. This exhibit was continued annually for 2 weeks prior to Easter and was enjoyed by many viewers. During this time, she was elected to be County Chairman of the Arts Program.

In 1955, she instructed 19 girls in the art of making dolls. The idea was very well received; and has been improved and has grown into the business she now operates.

As a youngster, she played with dolls that were made by the mothers using rags.

She started making her own dolls by stuffing and coloring them until she developed some that were very life-like. This was the beginning of her interest in creating Negro dolls.

She then took courses in doll-making and discovered that there wasn't a truly representative Negro doll. This encouraged her to create a doll that truly reflects all the Negro features.

She then sought a factory that produces Negro dolls and didn't find any in existence in the U.S., up until then, dolls were imported from abroad. The first doll company was set up here in 1910. It was thought that colored dolls would not appeal to Negro children. This was a misconception that has since been disproved. In many areas poor children could not afford real dolls—only the wealthy children had them.

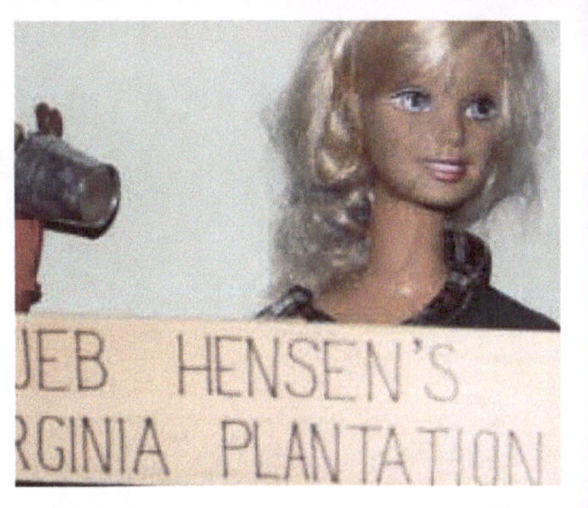

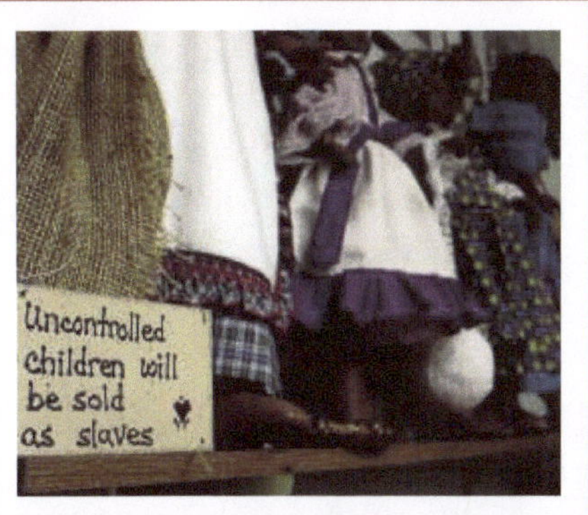

The first doll company was set up in 1910. It was thought that colored dolls would not appeal to Negro children.

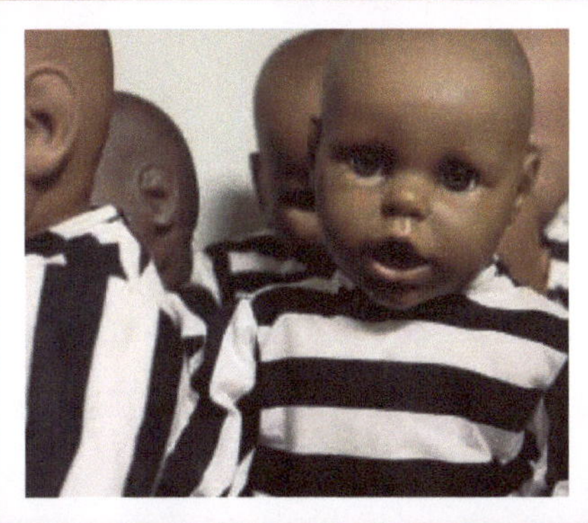

Today, dolls are produced at very reasonable rates, which are accessible to all children. Children relate to dolls very well and they help to develop the child's mental and social areas, as children are very imaginative. Dolls are a symbol of love and beauty.

She prided herself in having developed many natural looking dolls and stuffed toys, which have been copy-righted. She hoped they would be perpetuated for a long time to come, abroad.

Yia Eason, an African American businesswoman and mother, founded Olmec Toys, Inc., in 1985 when she realized that the toy industry provided no Black superhero toys for her three-year-old son to play with.

Eason, a Harvard M.B.A. graduate, felt impelled to act. Thus, she created what has become a $2.9 million business in just eight years.

Sun-Man, a superhero action figure and the Bronze Bombers, a troop of 33 4" action figures, fashioned after an ethnic army unit from World War I and II, were the first products introduced by Olmec.

Since 1990, Olmec has received financial, marketing, and technical assistance from Hasbro, Inc., the world's largest toy manufacturer. In 1993, Olmec's inventory was expanded to include 26 products, including heroic action figures, fashion dolls, cuddle baby dolls, and accessories.

How did Olmec Toy's get its name? Yia Eason named the company after an ancient Mexican civilization that sculptured 6-foot-high stone heads of Africans who came as traders to South America. These stone heads date back to 1600 B.C.

To My People

Marginalization of Blacks in history has meant the neglect of their many outstanding achievements. Blacks have lived and accomplished wonderful things. All that was needed to know of their wonders was to examine their work, combine the accomplishments in a single museum, and then marvel over what they achieved within or beyond great adversities.

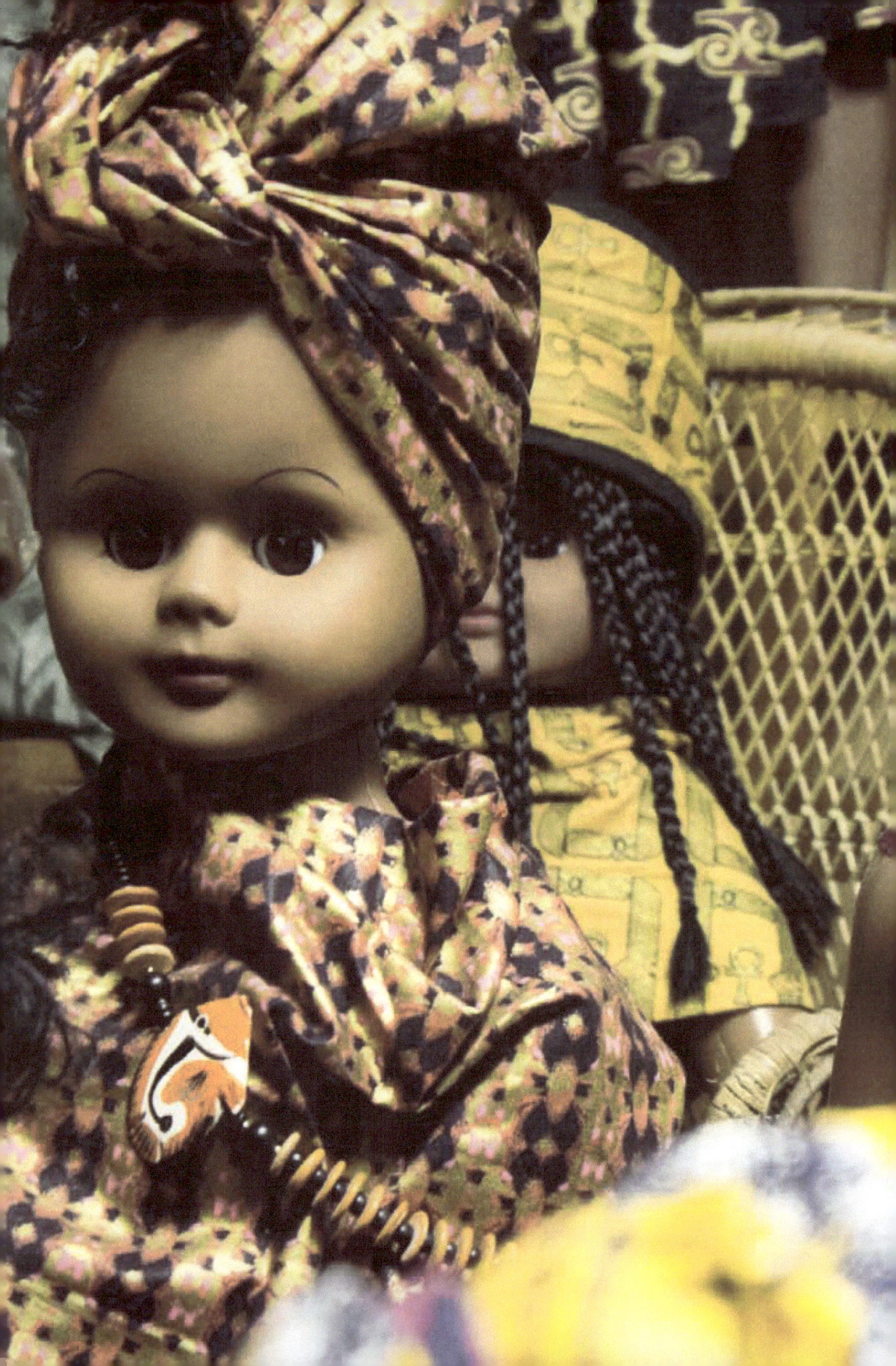

Where I Began

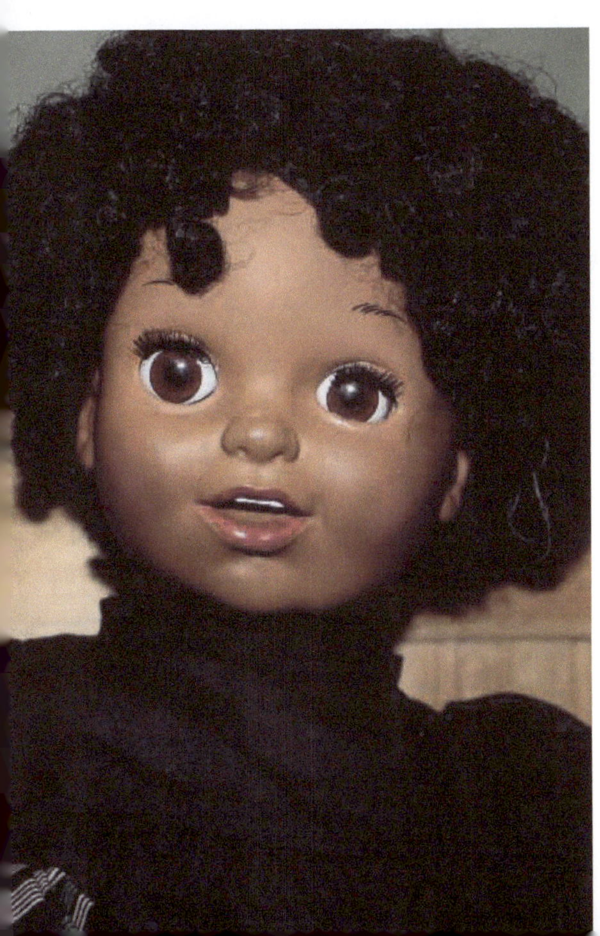

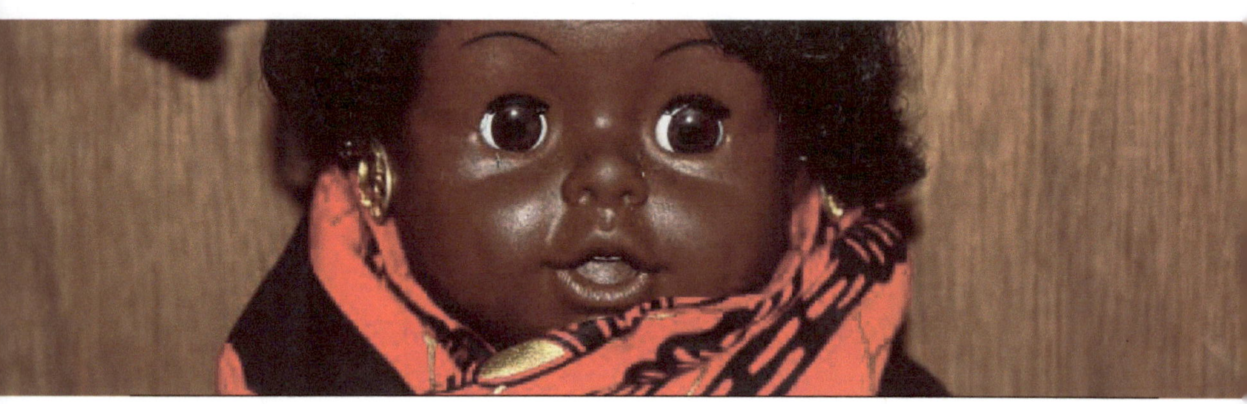

At the age of 12, I started reading and collecting African American Fiction and Nonfiction books—if I only would have kept the books and not let people read them, because they never gave them back. At that time I didn't keep an inventory of what I had or who borrowed the book. Today we can say we are the proud owners of over 2,000 African American books.

In 1979 at the age of 29, I started collecting dolls as an adult hobby. It started when I was in an old antique store and saw this dark-skinned dirty baby doll sitting on a shelf in the corner. She was so dirty. However, she caught my attention/eye, she was cute with dimples.

Her hair was very nappy and matted to her head. I said to myself, "she is happy to be nappy." I took her home and fixed her up and made an outfit for her.

This doll is the heart of my collection. This is the only doll that I never named. But we can call her "Nappy Happy".

The next thing I knew I gave her a mother who we named "Ms. Happy Nappy" and now she has over 3000 family members and friends to keep her company.

As a doll collector, I fell in love with African American dolls because they reflect my history and culture. The dolls have become a significant part of my life.

My best memories of the last 29 years are highlighted by dolls. I can't seem to get enough of them.

Just take a moment and really look at the expressions on doll faces. They really do look like real people. Each doll is unique and has its own personality and name.

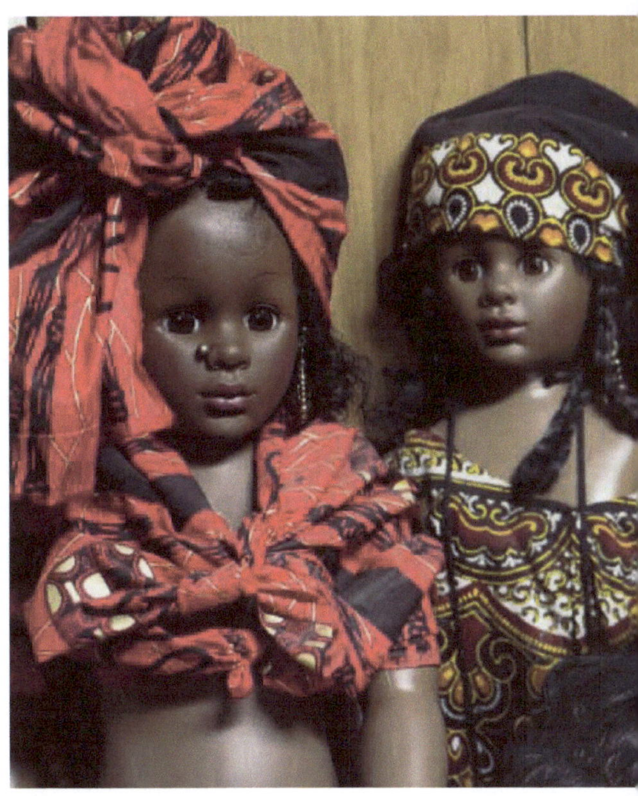

To me, there is no ugly doll; they all look good to me. I plan to collect dolls for many years to come. Because the dolls represent humanness, they seem to link us to one another.

A real bond has developed between the dolls and me.

I can't think of anything I would rather do. Each day God grants me a "new beginning". It is with this knowledge, acceptance, and understanding that the doors to my creativity continue to open. I am excited about what this year holds for me. Certainly, new beginnings lie ahead, complete with new blessings of creativity that's far beyond my scope of understanding.

The art of doll collecting has been extremely therapeutic and a great healing source for me. Year-after-year, I continue to collect dolls, but I am running out of room to put them. If it is the will of the Creator, you will see us in a museum in the state of Delaware one day.

> "In 1979 at the age of 29, I started collecting dolls as an adult hobby. It started when I was in an old antique store and saw this dark-skinned dirty baby doll sitting on a shelf in the corner."

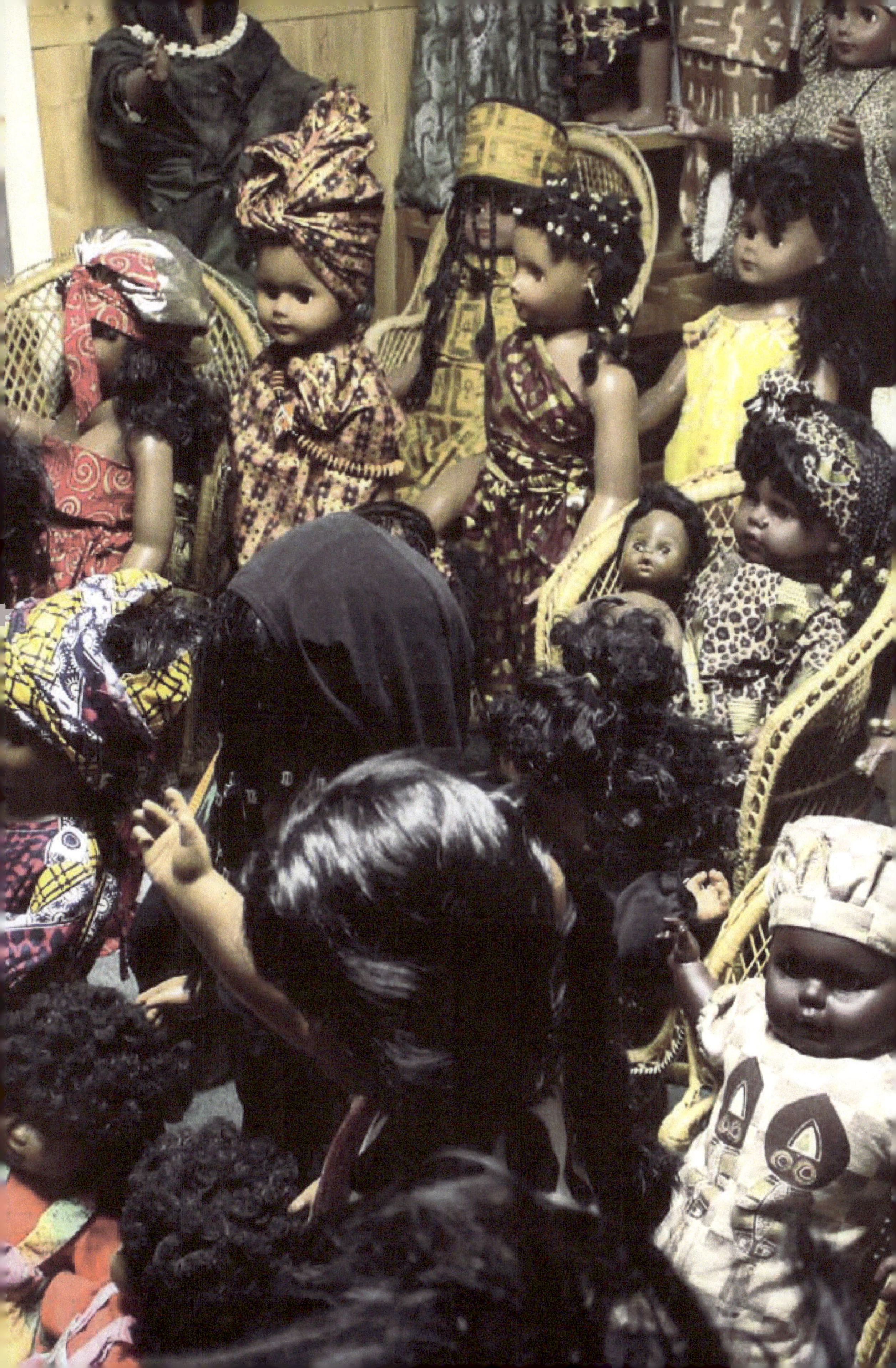

The Vision

Brown-Mosely's African American Heritage Museum

"No Longer Hidden, No Longer Ashamed!"

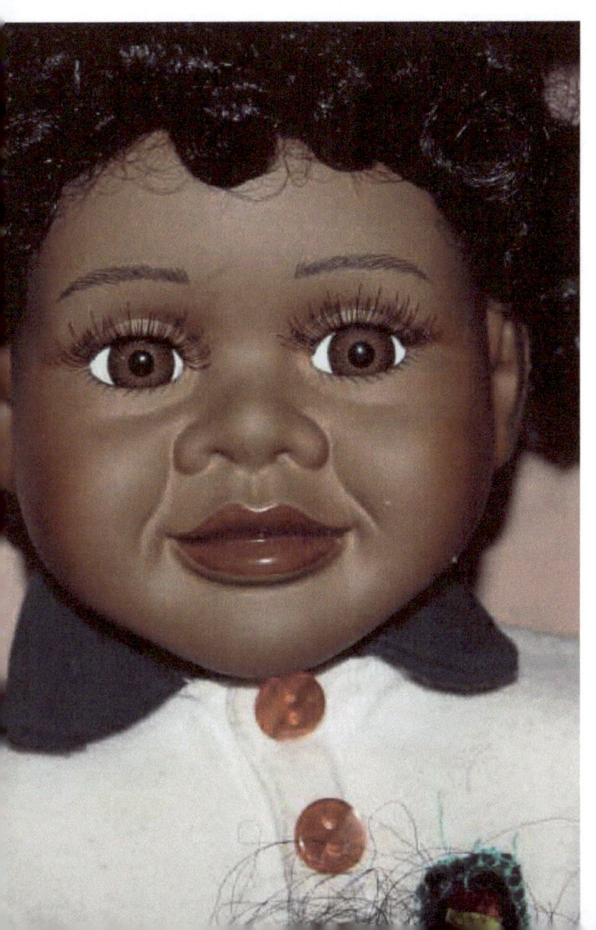

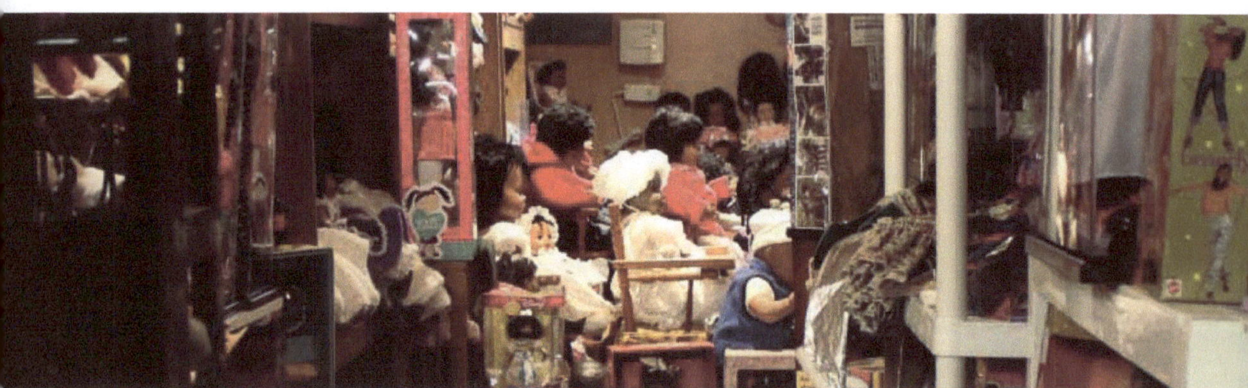

Why do I want to open an African American Doll Museum?

The enrichment of the lives of youth was a primary motivation for wanting to open a museum. Youth can begin serving at the museum at an early age and continue in various positions, as they grow older. The museum will offer opportunities for youth in and outside the community to take part in volunteer training programs, often providing a safe haven for at-risk youths.

I am blessed to have this dream and I am patiently waiting in having my dream fulfilled. I know one day I will be saying, "Thank You!" to God, the higher power, who grants all dreamers the courage to dream.

There are now, frankly, too many Dolls and African American Artifacts to comfortably fit in the Mosely house in Newark, Delaware. For the house, it's an enviable challenge to overcome—too many African American heroes, with more on the way.

We wanted to open this museum and put it in the hands of our people, as a testament to our individual power and reminder of our higher purpose. No people on earth have suffered as gravely or for as long as we have. But we have survived, and here we are, privileged ones for whom the generation before us sacrificed, struggled and kept the faith.

A museum about Black achievement is critical now, because everything that our forebears wanted for their children can now be ours. We have arrived at that moment in our history they so hoped for. Everything we need to live fully, everything necessary to our individual well-being and the well-being of our families and our communities, lies waiting for us to claim.

We must believe in ourselves and in the boundless ability God has given us to revive and renew ourselves emotionally, physically and spiritually along the way.

This museum is a tribute to the historical contribution of people of African descent. We want fellow human beings across the globe to know and never forget that here, in this colossal American empire and past American century, lived a great people of color who walked with much dignity and discernible effect to be true to themselves and their ideals of freedom against overwhelming odds and adverse circumstances.

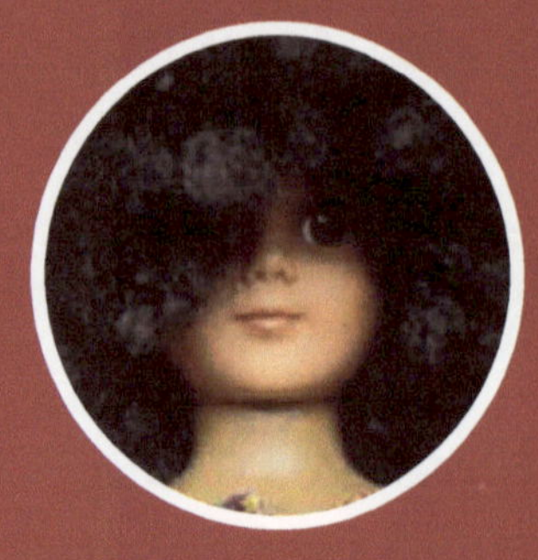

Angela Davis
Known as a radical African American educator, activist for civil rights and issues surrounding the private prisons. She is currently a professor at the University of California-Santa Cruz.

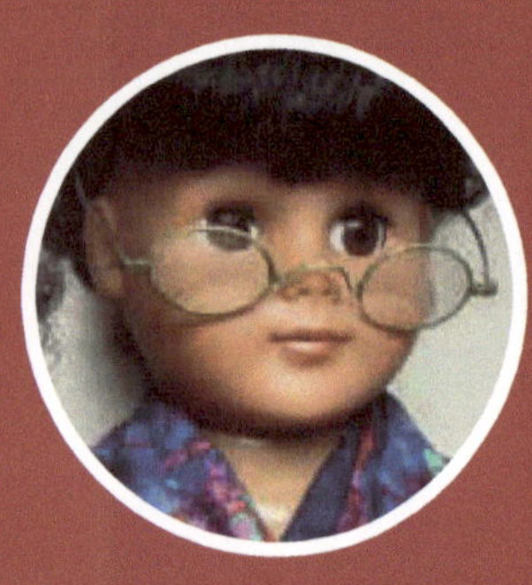

Rosa Parks
A civil rights activist, born on February 4, 1913 in Tuskegee, Alabama. Known for her refusal to surrender her seat to a White passenger on a Montgomery, Alabama bus spurred a city-wide boycott.

And, we especially want our granddaughters Rosa Marie and Nyesa Gabrielle, and all children, to remember that more democracy is always a possibility if they are willing to carry on the precious heritage with vision, courage, and compassion.

We come on behalf of our granddaughters and all people of African American decent, as we stretch across the ocean to the continent of Africa back to great-grandmothers and great grandfathers and great-great great-great-greats, and on and on, all the way back to the beginning of human life on earth.

Our effort and love stretches outward to fathers, mothers, brothers, sisters, uncles, aunts, nephews, nieces, cousins, grandfathers and grandmothers—a long and wide family procession.

The Mosely African American Doll Collection traces the evolution of Black Dolls, in various shades of African American Skin Tones. Our mission is to preserve the heritage, legacy, history of Black dolls and to research Black dolls.

A Teaching Tool

More than play toys, in fact, dolls are the first introduction of diversity/ difference to children. Some of the dolls symbolize the struggle for freedom and human dignity.

Children relate to dolls very well. Dolls help to develop the child's mental and social areas as children are very imaginative. Dolls are a symbol of love and beauty.

As we relate to our various skin tones, the doll will help little boys and girls to embrace themselves and not be ashamed of whom God created them to be, but to be proud and pleased about whom God made them to be.

The growth and legacy of Black dolls will increase as artists continue to design and create beautiful Black dolls.

Our doll collection and museum will show interest in mannerisms and education, coupled with a fierce determination to: "Train up a child in the way they should go". (Proverbs 22:6)

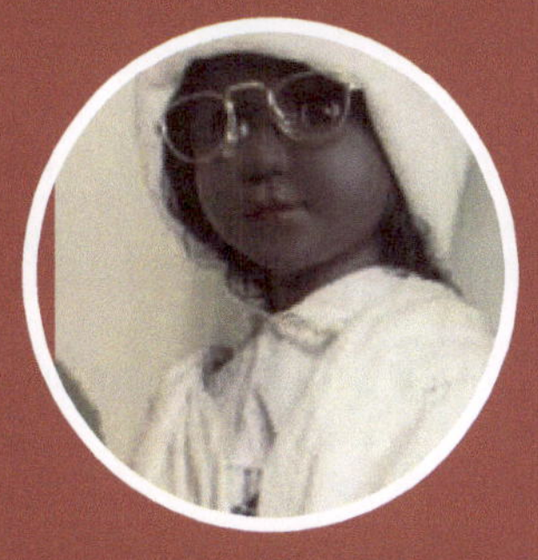

Sojourner Truth
Born Isabella Baumfree in 1797. Sojourner Truth was the self-given name. Known as an African American abolitionist and women's rights activist with her speech on racial inequalities, "Ain't I a Woman?"

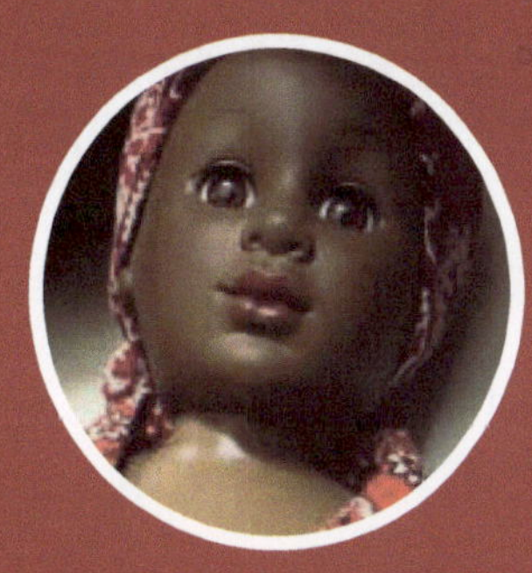

Cicely Tyson
Born December 19, 1933 in Harlem, NY. Tyson has won two Emmys, among other awards, over the course of her acting career. She was also inducted into the Black Filmmakers Hall of Fame.

Children will carefully be drilled in protocol and proper social graces, along with learning meal planning, sewing, and the proper things to do, to say, to wear, etc.

365 Days of Black History through Dolls

This concept conveys the experience of African Americans through a theme that unites strikingly different groups and individuals. We spotlight those whose lives brought change to America, whether through their musical genius, their public service, their unconventional thinking, or some other means.

> "CHILDREN RELATE TO DOLLS VERY WELL AND THEY HELP TO DEVELOP THE CHILD'S MENTAL AND SOCIAL AREAS AS CHILDREN ARE VERY IMAGINATIVE. DOLLS ARE A SYMBOL OF LOVE AND BEAUTY."

The growth and legacy of Black dolls will increase as artists continue to design and create beautiful Black dolls.

The Mosely African American Doll Collection contains a wealth of information on us. It includes the following:

- People: Civil Rights Leaders and Civil Rights Era, important scholars, scientists, artists, explorers, politicians, athletes and slavery.
- Places: The nations and major cities of Africa.
- Culture: The Harlem Renaissance, the Fisk Jubilee Singers, Trailblazers, the Negro Baseball League, Gospel, Jazz, Rhythm, Blues and Rap.

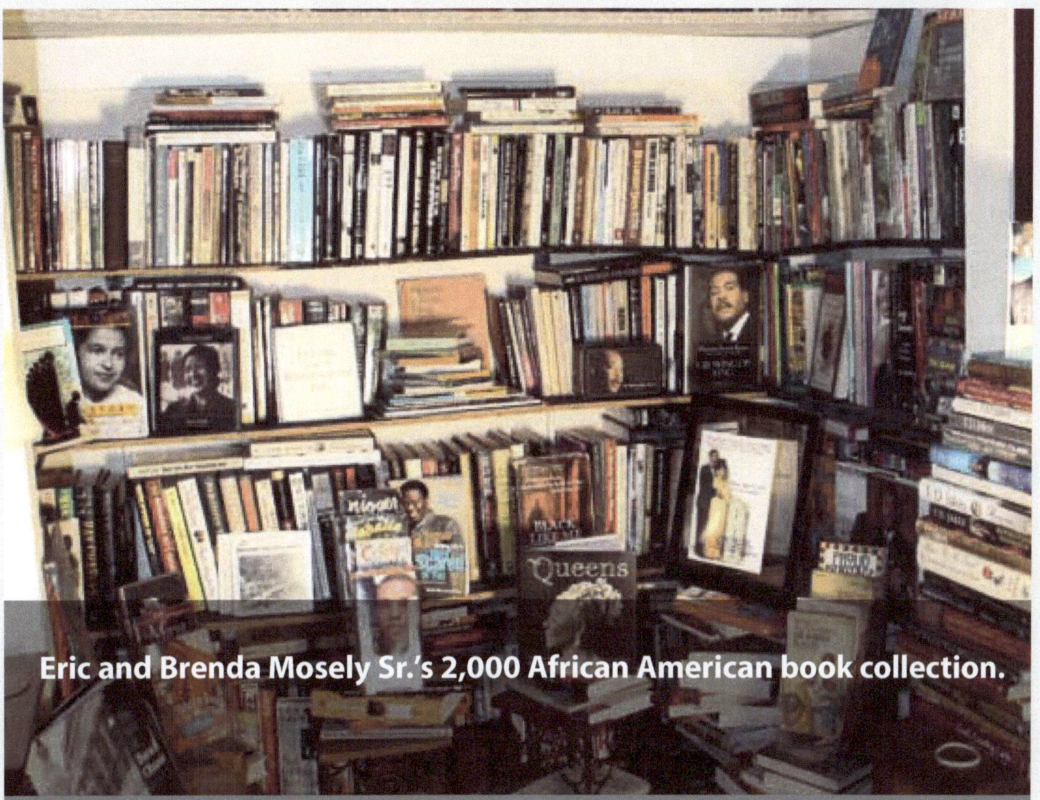

Eric and Brenda Mosely Sr.'s 2,000 African American book collection.

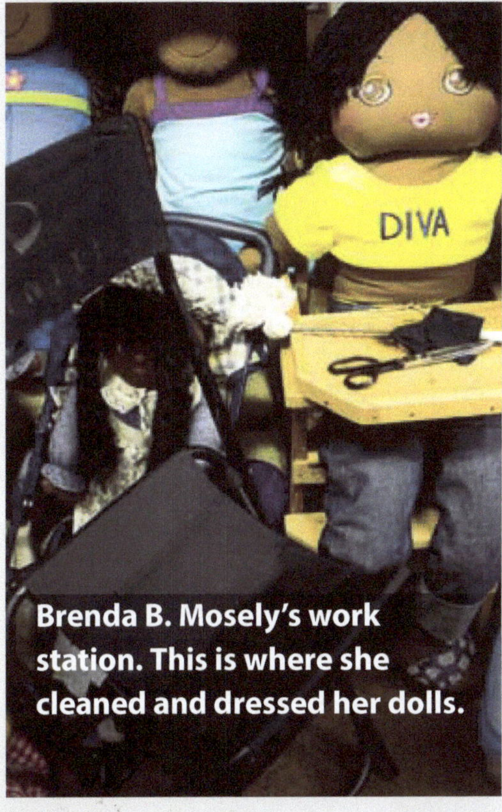

Brenda B. Mosely's work station. This is where she cleaned and dressed her dolls.

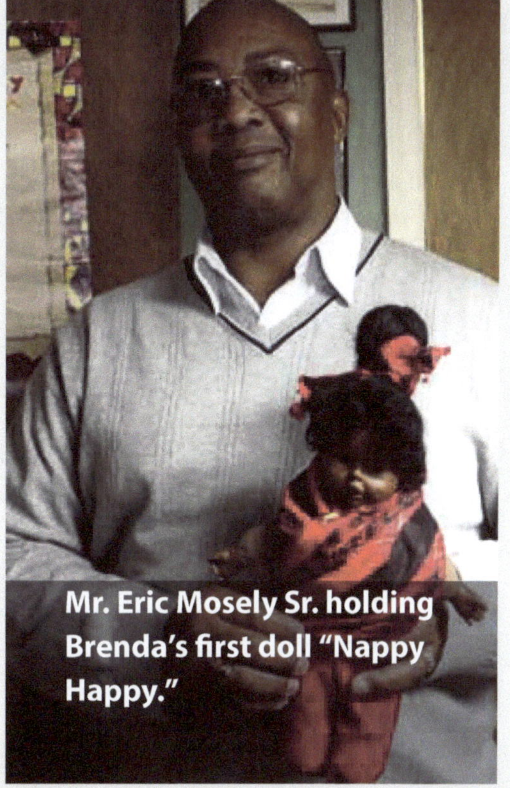

Mr. Eric Mosely Sr. holding Brenda's first doll "Nappy Happy."

- Politics: Political groups, movements and events, including the 1963 March on Washington. The voting rights struggle, Birmingham church bombing and the victory over apartheid of the African national congress.

- History: The major events of the African American past, including resistance to slavery, the abolitionists and the civil rights movement.

It would be difficult to find a significant area of African American dolls and history–from slavery to science, from music to the military, from civil rights to sports, from the Million Man March to extraordinary and ordinary everyday life–that is not covered in the Mosely African American Doll Collection.

With over 65 displays/exhibits and readable, concise entries perfect for easy reference, as well as for browsing, the Mosely African American Doll Collection covers significant events, people, terms, ideas, and social movements that are part of the rich African American Heritage.

We celebrate the accomplishments of African American men, women, and communities throughout centuries of history. From the first slaves through the abolitionists, the Harlem Renaissance, the battle for civil rights, and today.

Our doll exhibits touch on all aspects of the rich history of our African American heritage and our contribution in areas such as:

- Civil Rights and Politics: Including the accomplishments of Frederick Douglass, Sojourner Truth, Martin Luther King, Jr., Reverend Jesse Jackson, and Kweisi Mfume.

- The Arts: Including Toni Morrison, Miles Davis, Stevie Wonder, and Alvin Ailey, as well as important books, film, and works of art.
- Science and Medicine: Includes Daniel Hale Williams, the first person to perform a successful open-heart operation, and Rebecca Lee, the first African American woman to receive a medical degree.
- Religion: Covers the First African Baptist Church in Savannah, Georgia to the Nation of Islam.
- Sports: Covers many sports, from baseball to football, and includes the accomplishments of Jackie Robinson, Muhammad Ali, Arthur Ashe, Jackie Joyner-Kersee, and others.

The Mosely African American Doll Collection is the ultimate survey of all things African American, from major names and events to more obscure and lesser-known individuals and facts.

Each person profiled in this collection was and is just like us—a life filled with unending challenges and changes. Like the sisters and brothers in this doll collection, we have to clear away the subconscious patterns and beliefs that undermine our best intentions and weaken our trust in the essential goodness of life.

We must learn to embrace our own people, our power and our intuition; we must never fear change. Instead, we must stay committed to learning, to finding the lessons in change, even as we devise new strategies for moving forward.

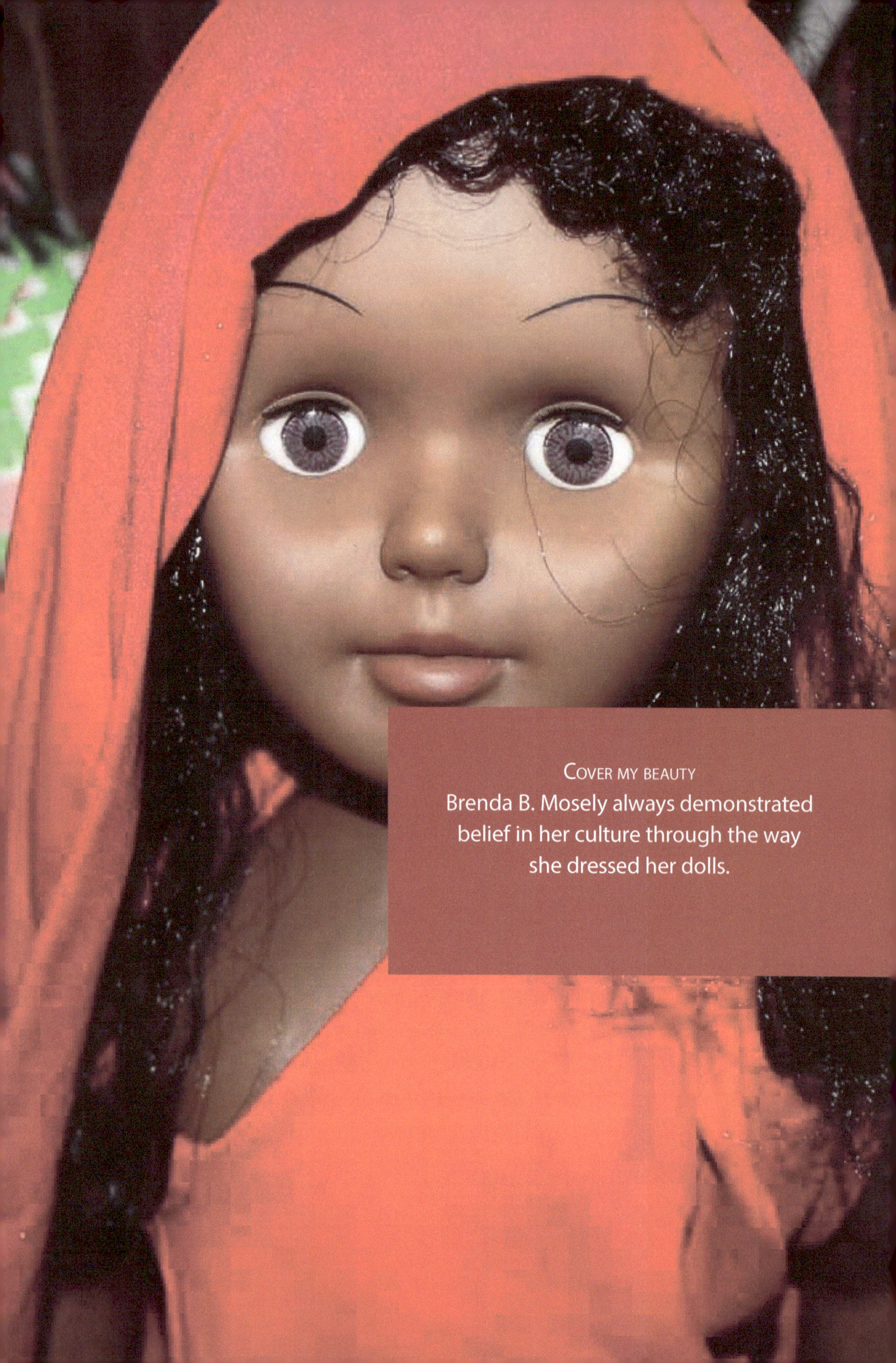
Cover my beauty
Brenda B. Mosely always demonstrated belief in her culture through the way she dressed her dolls.

It is our hope that the display and stories in this museum and companion books will inspire us to keep growing and moving forward in our lives. It is our hope that, through the example of all of these extraordinary women and men, we may find our own power and purpose, and the conviction that—"together we can achieve the happiness and prosperity God has promised us, in a world of everlasting peace".

African American Children Development

When I went to elementary and junior high school, they didn't teach us anything about African Americans. When I was in high school, they didn't teach us anything about African Americans except in February during Black History Month. At our museum, we will do it every day and week. This is important to me.

Parents and educators will agree that Black children who take classes and attend Afrocentric schools and museums exhibit genuine enthusiasm for learning that translates into high academic achievement.

And, because they are routinely exposed to the richness of African American culture, the children develop a strong sense of self-esteem that helps counter negative societal messages about Black people. At our museum, we will celebrate Heritage Day, dressing as Black historical figures and giving speeches.

In addition to the federal Martin Luther King, Jr. holiday, the museum will also honor the birthdays of Harriet Tubman, Frederick Douglass, Sojourner Truth, W.E.B. DuBois, Marcus Garvey, and Malcolm X.

At our museum, we will strive for excellence in our quest to be the best. We will rise above every challenge with our heads held high. We'll always keep the faith when others doubt. We'll march on till victory is ours.

Our museum will also open the doors of self-esteem by presenting young African Americans with positive role models and achievable possibilities. It portrays individuals and organizations that are making important contributions to the Black community and to American culture, as a whole.

> "WE MUST LEARN TO EMBRACE OUR OWN PEOPLE AND POWER AND INTUITION; WE MUST NEVER FEAR CHANGE."

Our museum says, in effect, that there can be a comfortable synthesis of African and American values, and that this reconciliation is essential to American society.

African Americans celebrate not only the successful and famous among us, but also the everyday heroes: effective community organizations and the invaluable cooperative spirit of the African American community.

The Mosely African American Doll Collection presents not only a rich community heritage, but a real basis for pride in present day African American accomplishments and real hope for the future.

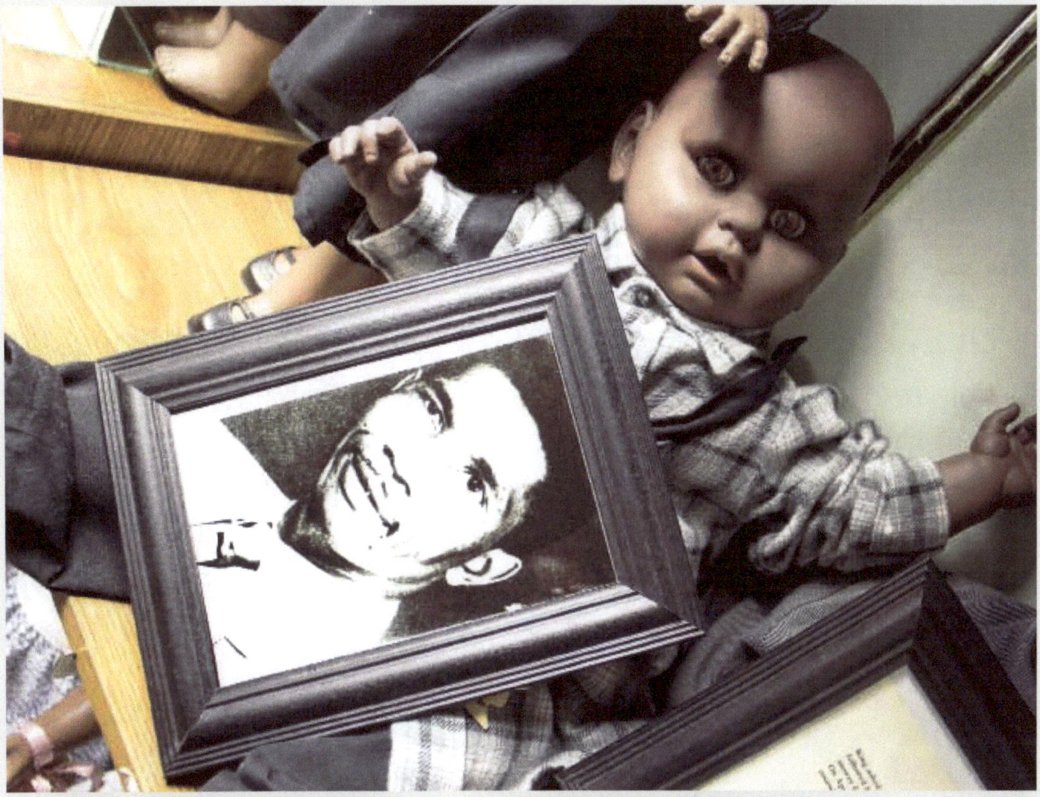

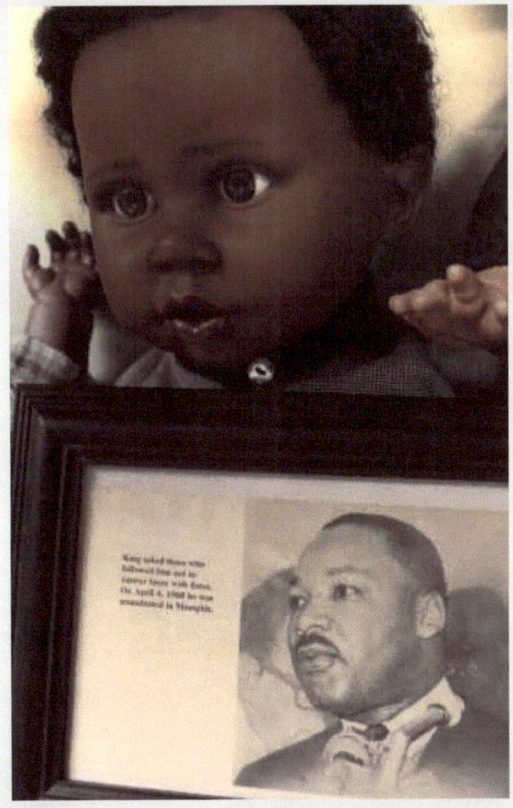
King asked those who
followed him not to
answer force with force.
On April 4, 1968 he was
assassinated in Memphis.

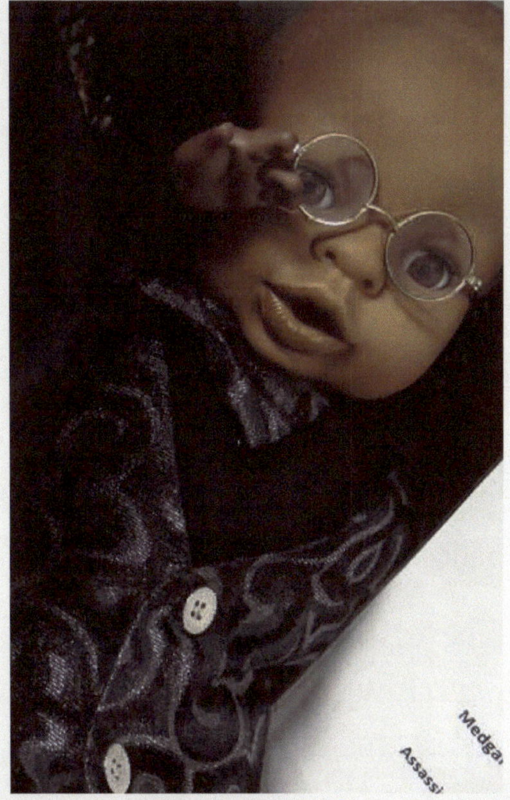

Getting the Most Out of This Museum

As it is not possible to include all of the African American people and events that have helped to shape history, we want to use this museum to encourage people to do their own research and investigations, adding to the timeline through the years.

Beautiful selections of art, books, décor, and dolls highlight a people and events that have contributed to our nation's diversity and civil and human rights.

We accept contributions and donations. Anyone can add more people and events, using their own collections of art, books, décor, dolls, essays, and photos, with names and dates.

A Caution for People Visiting the Museum

All entries had to be documented, using several sources of information, when possible. Many sources gave conflicting information, and at times, it was clear that the information was simply incorrect. We have to call for a wider search to attempt to resolve conflicting histories. We encourage all visitors to notify us when errors are found.

History of Black Dolls

The Mosely African American Doll Collection, with its history of Black dolls by no means includes every Black doll made. There are many, many more Black dolls yet to be located, documented and placed in the museum.

The task of finding these dolls will be work. Searching, more searching, and much more searching, this is the procedure and it makes me happy.

Doll Names

Nothing is as personal or meaningful as a name. A name can reveal history, identity, and cultural distinctiveness. Names can have positive or negative meanings.

This has been particularly true as we have struggled over 200 years to find a name that captures the essence of being American of African descent. God takes names seriously.

The Bible tells us. "He counts the stars and call them all by name..." Psalm 147:4. As you journey through the museum, you will notice each doll has a name.

The history of Black Dolls and Tracing Doll Roots

The Black doll is a teaching tool as we relate to our various skin tones. The dolls will help little girls and boys to embrace themselves and not be ashamed of whom God created them to be but to be proud of whom God made them to be regardless of their skin tone.

Donations

Children and adults will be encouraged to donate their dolls for display when they no longer want to play with them. Their name will be displayed on the exhibit. When the doll was made, what is the doll's name and how old is the doll.

American Manufactured

This includes various dolls, which were made in the 1920-1930s when most white molded dolls were painted brown or black. Small tufts of yarn could be added for hair.

Amosandra, dressed in a red and white checkered dress, is a rubber baby doll that represents the daughter of Amos, from the CBS radio show, Amos and Andy.

This doll came with its own birth certificate, which dates 1949. Since the late fifties, there has been an increase of Black dolls on the markets.

And since the civil rights movement of the 60's, there has been an increase in the number of Black doll manufacturers to produce ethnically correct dolls for African American families.

Dressed in a yellow and white organdy dress, wearing a matching hat, is the first ethnically corrected doll made by Ideal Doll Company. She is made of vinyl and cloth and her name is Sara lee. Her creator is Sara Lee Creech from Belle Glade, Florida, who thought that Negro children should have a doll that looked like them.

The Sara Lee doll is a celebrity because first lady Eleanor Roosevelt, Ralph Bunche, the NAACP and many prominent persons endeared her.

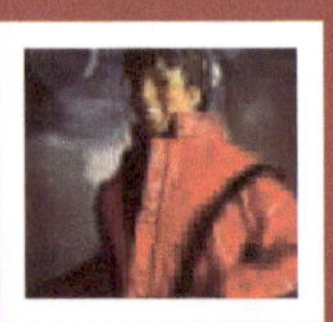

Michael Jackson Doll

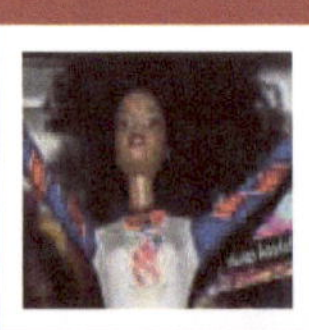

Female Athlete Dolls

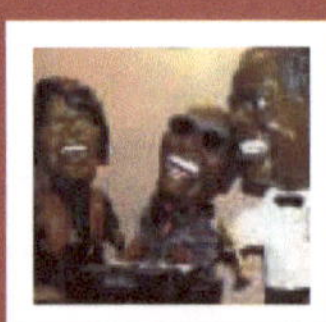

James Brown, Ray Charles & Louis Armstrong Dolls

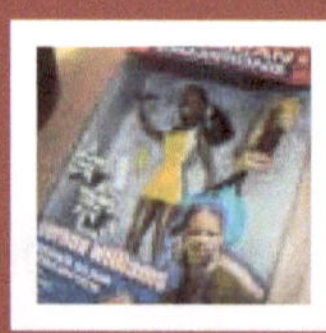

Serena & Venus Doll

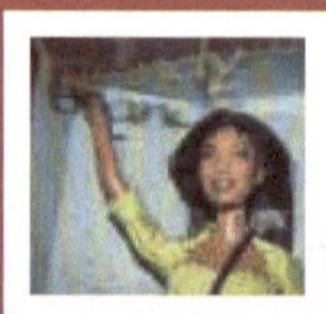

Brandy Doll

Research Library

The research library will offer a collection of books on African American history, art, décor, and doll history, doll making, doll artists and doll encyclopedias. Videos and back issues of doll magazines will be available for research and enjoyment.

Membership

As a member of the Mosely African American Doll Collection museum, you will join with others who share an appreciation of history and culture through African American art, books, décor and especially dolls.

Also, you will be able to participate in the following:

- Africa, Black History Activity
- Reading Room & Story Time
- Lessons on the Civil Rights Movement
- Trips to Historic Landmarks
- Doll Shows, Doll Coloring, and Doll Dressing Contests

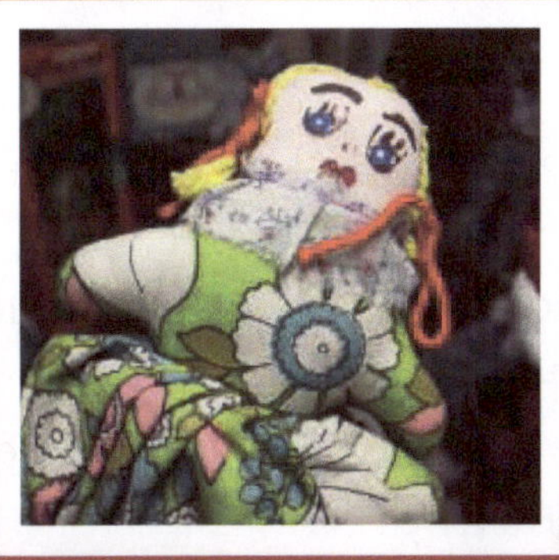

Topsy Turvy Doll Collection

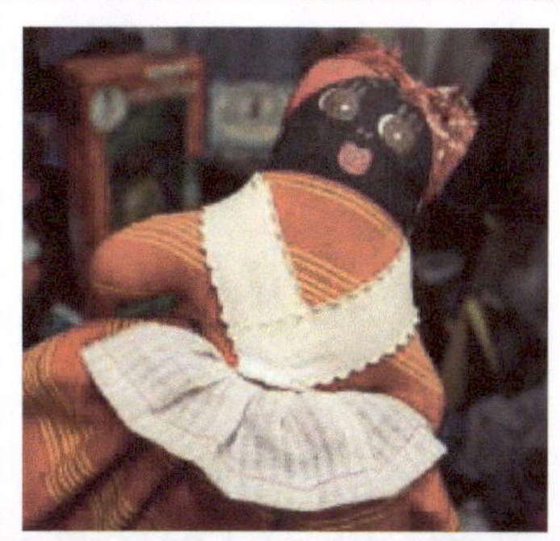

- Visit to other Doll museums
- Tracing our doll roots through people who have had dolls made after them

Employment/Jobs (Volunteers) for Youth and Senior Citizens

- Admission/Cashiers , Work in Gift shop
- Youth Responsibility mentoring younger children
- Youth host and hostess at the award dinners and parties
- Tour Guides
- Crochet & Sewing Instructors
- Contest Judges
- Workshop Facilitators/Leaders
- Teachers

Cultural Workshops

The journey into the doll world will begin at the age of five. A child has to be able to do something useful, I would say. By the time that she is eight a girl should be able to crochet, sew, and cut paper patterns for clothes. She should also know how to keep herself well groomed. Additional activities for self and community development will include:

- African American History Lessons/Classes:
- Awards Dinner: Recognize individuals who have performed extraordinary service to enhance the life of our youth.
- Birthday Parties/Celebrations for the children

- Black History Month Programs
- Doll Making Workshops for children, teenagers and adults
- Doll Dressing Contest (Monthly)
- Essay Contest: On Art, Dolls, and our African American History
- Gift Shop
- Movie Room: video showings of Doll history and African American films
- Photography exhibitions of little girls and their dolls
- Lectures: activity and lessons
- Reading Room
- Story Time, Lessons on the Civil Rights Movement
- Story Time, Lessons on Dolls
- Tea Parties for little girls
- Tours to other African American Doll museums
- Tours to African American Bookstores, Libraries and Museums
- Tours for churches, daycares, boys and girls clubs, schools, orphanages, youth centers
- Trips to Historic African American Landmarks and other Museums

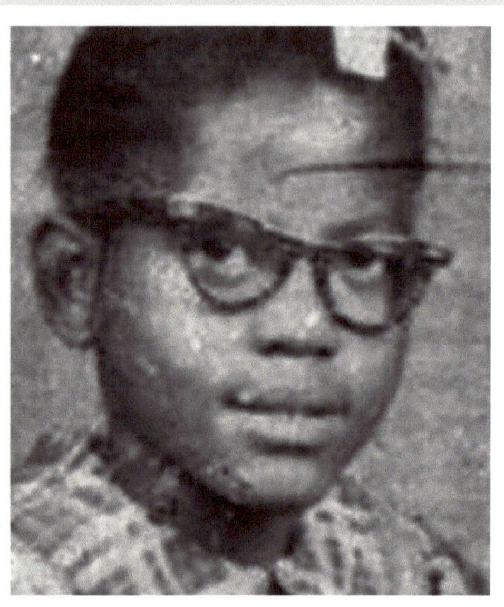

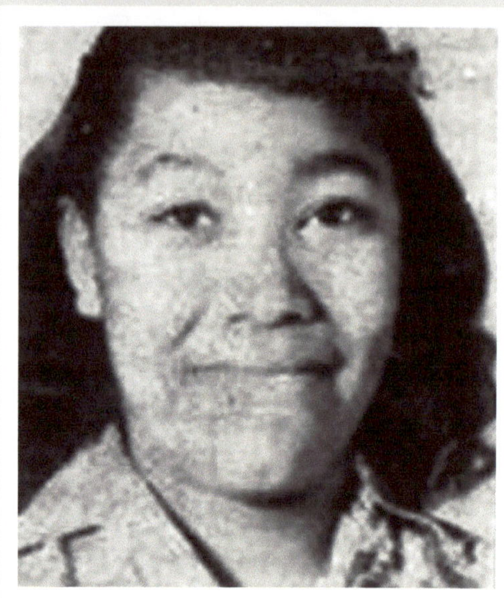

The four little girls

Addie Mae Collins, age 14, Denise McNair, age 11, Carole Robertson, age 14, and Cynthia Wesley, age 14, were getting ready to attend a youth service when they were killed by the bomb explosion.

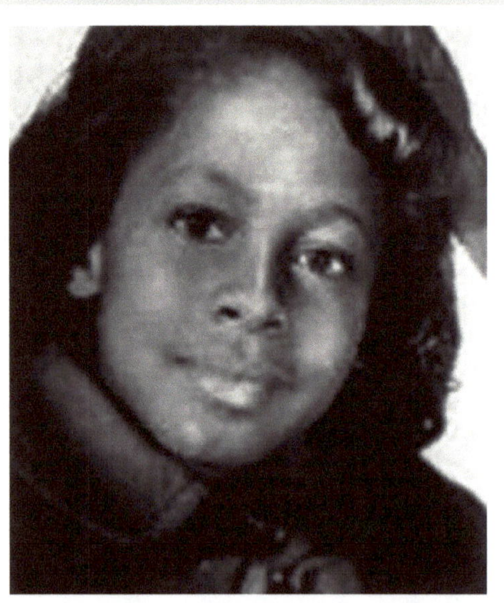

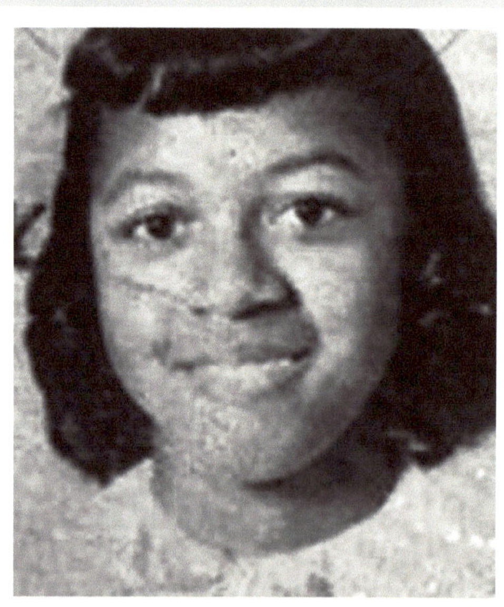

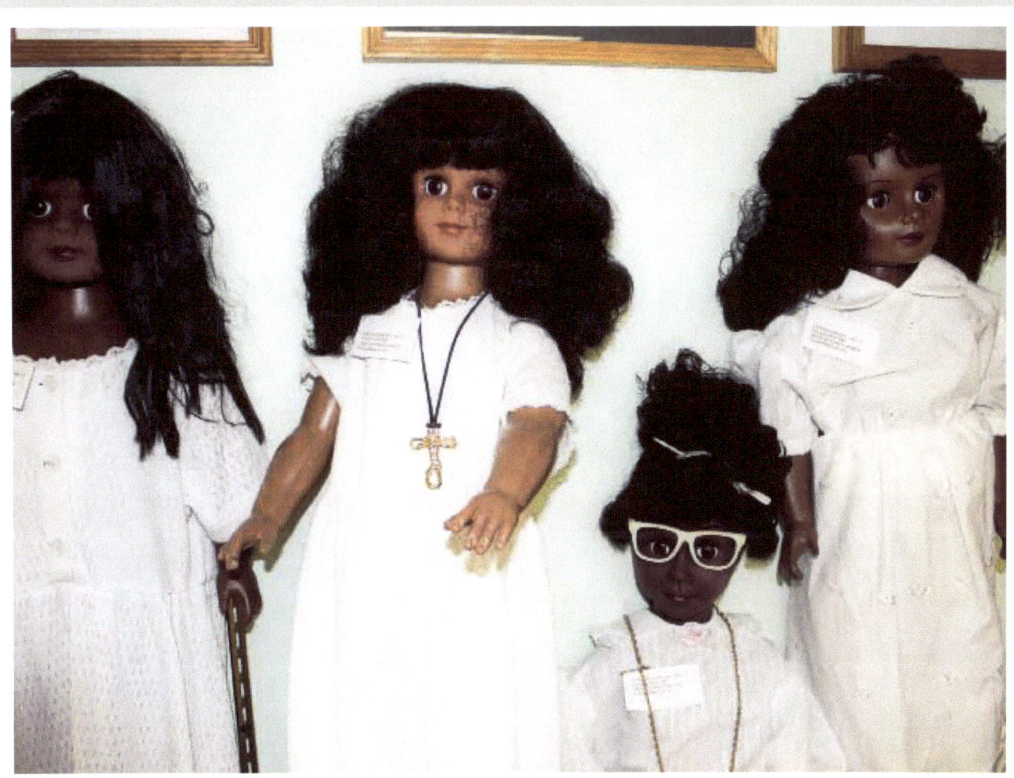

Birmingham Church Bombing

The Sept. 15, 1963, bombing at the Sixteenth Street Baptist Church in Birmingham, Alabama, was one of the most abhorrent crimes of the civil rights movement. Four young girls attending Sunday school—Denise McNair, Cynthia Wesley, Carole Robertson, and Addie Mae Collins, aged 11 to 14—were killed when a bomb exploded at the church. Twenty others were injured. The church was a center for civil rights meetings, and just a few days earlier, courts had ordered the desegregation of Birmingham's schools. Here is Brenda's dedicational doll replica of the four little girls.

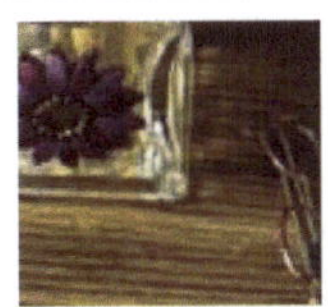

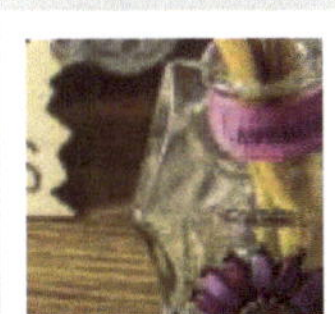

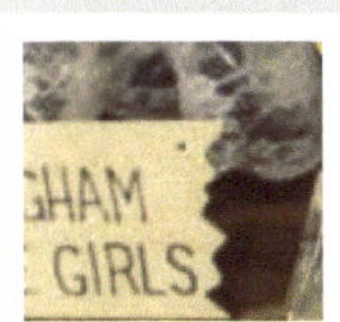

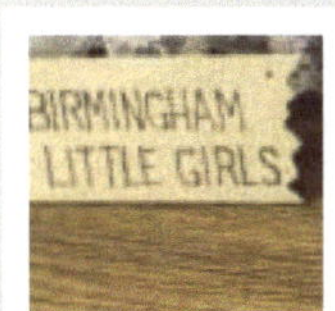

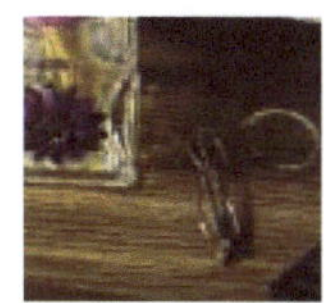

My Journey

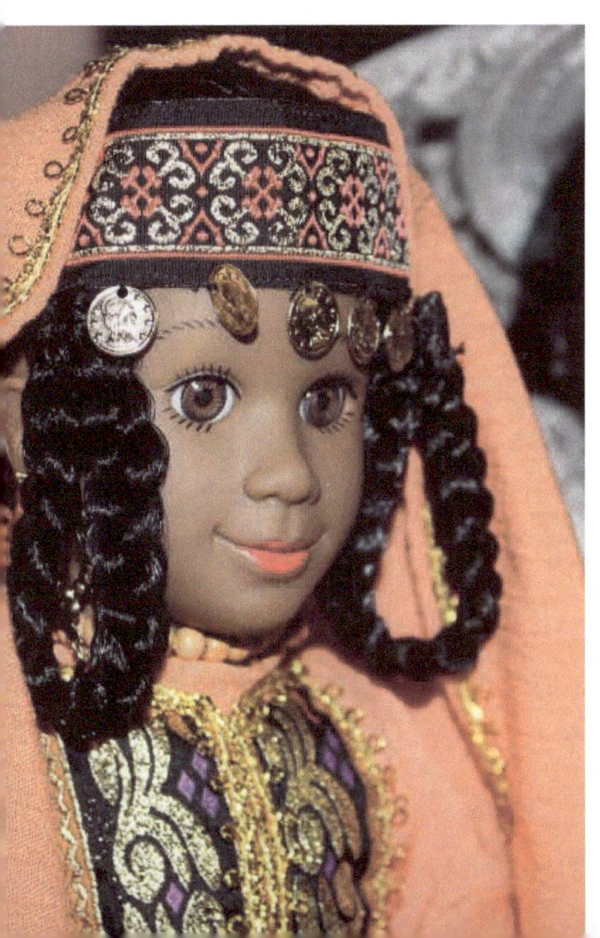

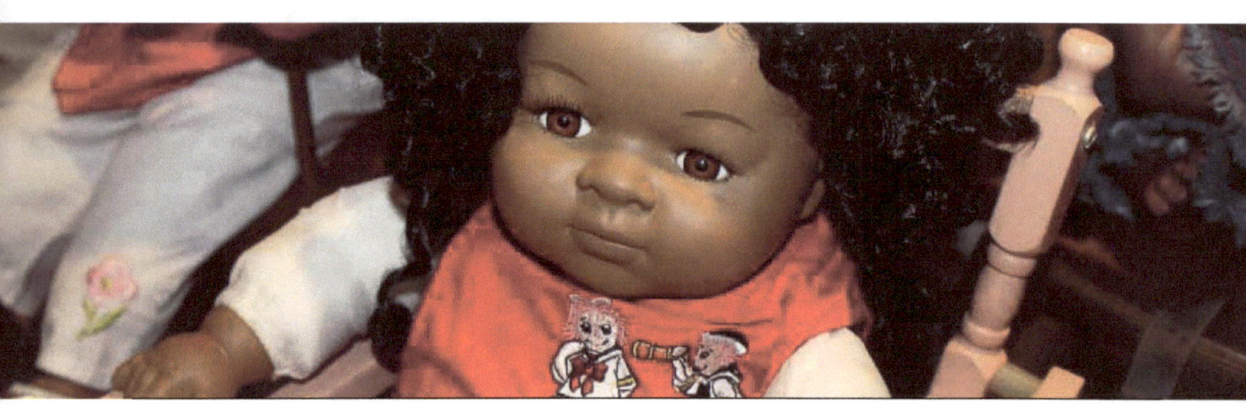

I was born on Saturday, April 22, 1950 in a house at 1711 W. Norris Street, Philadelphia, Pennsylvania. My parents were the late John Hollis and Mozelle Dowdy Brown. I am the ninth child of twelve siblings.

In the late 1950s, when I was a little girl growing up in an apartment at 1961 North Gratz Street in Philadelphia, we were very poor. However, I was enriched by my mother's love, kindness, gentleness, patience, and appreciation for all her children.

It was my mother who taught me the art of putting things together and who took me to work with her to show me how other people lived. She allowed me to go away from Friday to Sunday mornings to a White person's home in the better parts of Pennsylvania where I would baby-sit their two children, a boy and a girl.

The White couple went out on Friday and Saturday nights. Every Saturday afternoon they dropped me and the two children off at the movies, picked us up and cooked dinner for us (fish sticks and French fries). It was in this home where my dreams, desires and inspiration for having nice things came from. Because of where I lived, I was not fully aware of any other race except Black people and (Mr. Benny), the Jewish man that owned the corner store who gave us credit. From my neighbors, I saw and heard testimonials about the troubles of many poor people.

Somehow I didn't think about money. I would day-dream so often of having a big nice house, nice clothes and plenty of food to eat. I so believed in ideals and dreams. This big house that I dreamt of had a library of all Black books.

I decided on a rainy afternoon to run away from my home (in the ghetto) and go live in books, at the library and movies. By chance, the book I read and the movie I went to see was the first Black book and film I had ever seen, entitled "Carmen Jones".

As I sat amazed by Dorothy Dandridge's beautiful face, I realized the film and the actors were unlike any I had ever seen before. It was more than the fact that these were Black faces on the silver screen. Dorothy Dandridge and the other actors proved to be a source of inspiration. Therefore, for the duration of my childhood in the 1950s and throughout the 1960s, I found myself always on the lookout for books, and movies on television with Black faces.

From the old films on television, I caught glimpses of a variety of performers with such bizarre names as Stepin' Fetchin, Hattie McDaniel, Butterfly McQueen, Bojangles, Rochester, and Lena Horne. Sometimes at the local movie house, I had a brief introduction to

Sidney Poitier, Ruby Dee, and Ossie Davis.

As my interest in Black actors, movies, and books increased, I longed for more information about them—asking questions like: How many pictures has Stepin' Fetchin' made? Did Hattie McDaniel always play a servant? Was there a movie in which Bojangles did not dance?

The first book I came across and read, which was about actors, inventors and famous Black people, was titled "The First Book of American Negroes" by Margaret B. Young. I still have this book today.

> "I HAVE BEEN DEEPLY CONCERNED FOR MANY YEARS BY THE WAY AFRICAN AMERICANS FELL THROUGH THE CRACKS OF HISTORY..."

Seldom was I able to find answers to my questions. There was not one book in the library that I could borrow for information. Among play friends and my school mates, there was hardly any concern about a Black face other than Sidney Poitier, and when I dared mention a Fetchin' or a Rochester I was soon informed that these people were villains and betrayers; nothing more than Uncle Toms and handkerchief heads.

So I learned to keep my mouth shut about Black actors I really did care about. I still read and saw every Black film I could. This love continued through high school and all of my adult life.

I am an African American who has never, ever, ever been ashamed of who God created me to be and I always believed in myself; it is not that I am superior to anyone else, but simply believe that we, as African Americans, have great value and have made great contributions to the world.

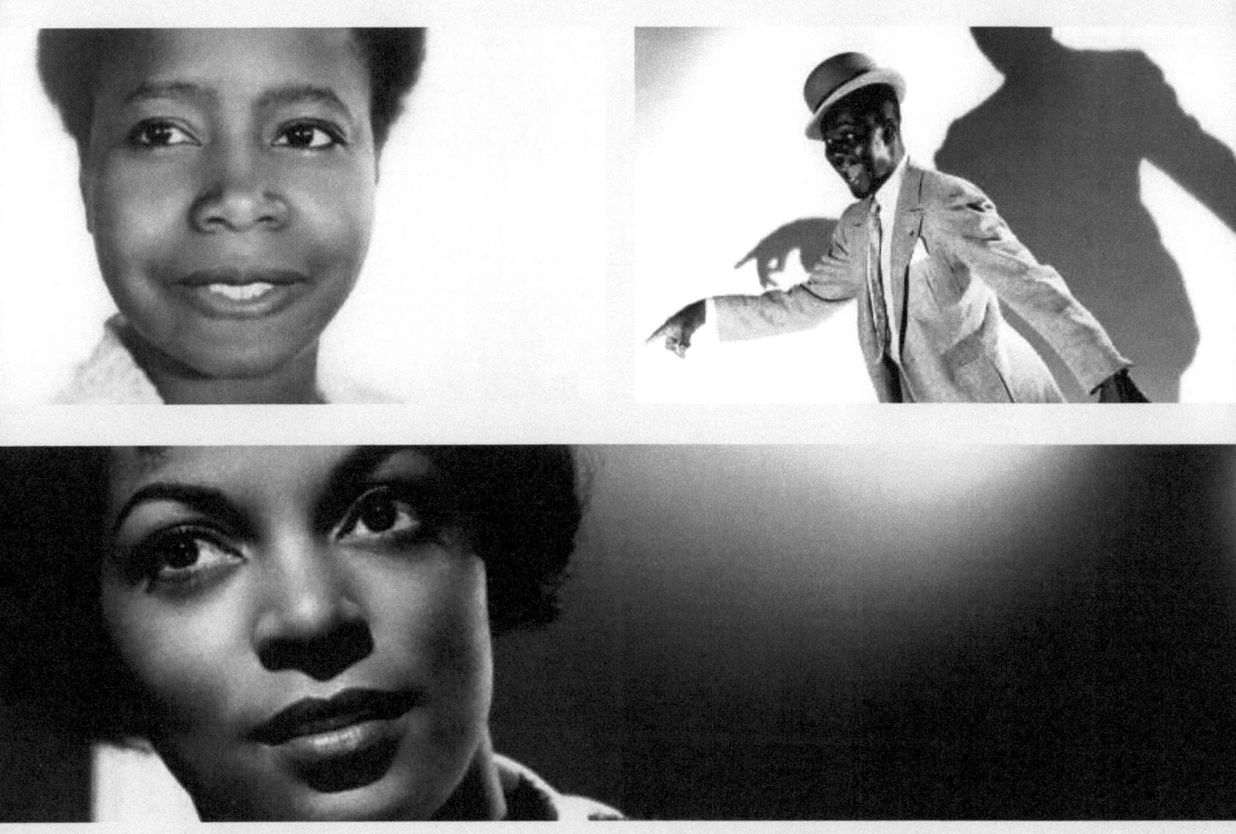

"The kind of beauty I want most is the hard-to-get kind that comes from within: strength, courage, dignity."
– Ruby Dee

Actress Ruby Dee, born Ruby Ann Wallace in Cleveland, Ohio in 1924, grew up in Harlem. She got involved in acting as a teenager and began studying her craft at the American Negro Theatre in 1941. She is well known for collaborations with her husband, actor Ossie Davis. Dee's films span a generation and include The Jackie Robinson Story in the 1950's, A Raisin in the Sun (1961) and Do the Right Thing in 1988. In 2008, Dee received her first Oscar nomination for playing Mama Lucas in the hit film American Gangster. She also attended Hunter College.

I find it sad, that still, African Americans are ashamed of being themselves. It's time to embrace our culture and feel proud to be different. I want little girls to know that they are beautiful no matter what color they are. I want to embrace young girls, to empower young girls and to help them see that there is nothing in this world they can't be.

I want to spread the word that BLACK is and always has been BEAUTIFUL, no matter the shade, no matter the skin tone. I can truly say that I have never been ashamed of who God created me to be. There is not one day in my life that I don't wake up proud to be a Beautiful African American Woman. If only I could make others feel this way—"Loving the Skin I'm In"!

I was told most of my life that Black people had no dolls other than rag dolls. Growing up, I remember only having one Black rag doll to play with. I began collecting proof that there were beautiful African American dolls made for Black children, and I started this doll museum so that everyone could see the beautiful Black babies that come in all shades of color and skin tones.

I am a civil rights activist and a collector of African American art, books, decor, dolls, literature and movies.

And, yes I am a member of the NAACP, ARE YOU?

I am very proud of my ethnicity and heritage. I am a historian, or some may say, scholar of our African American history. I have been documenting the history and contributions of African Americans for many years.

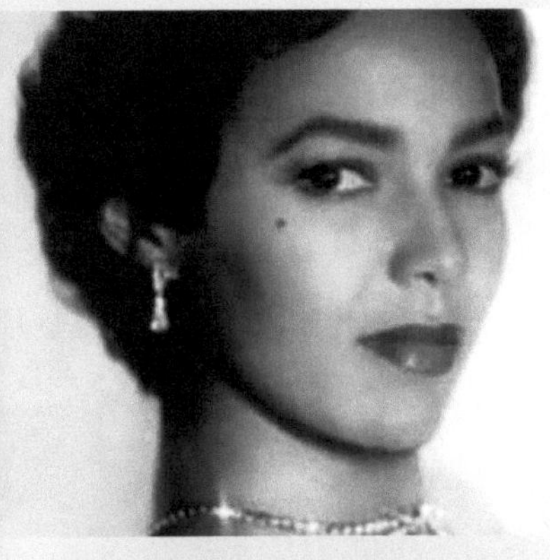

Born November 9, 1922 in Cleveland, Ohio, Dorothy Dandridge sang at Harlem's Cotton Club and Apollo Theatre and became the first African American woman to be nominated for an Academy Award for best actress. Many years passed before the mainstream entertainment industry acknowledged Dandridge's legacy.

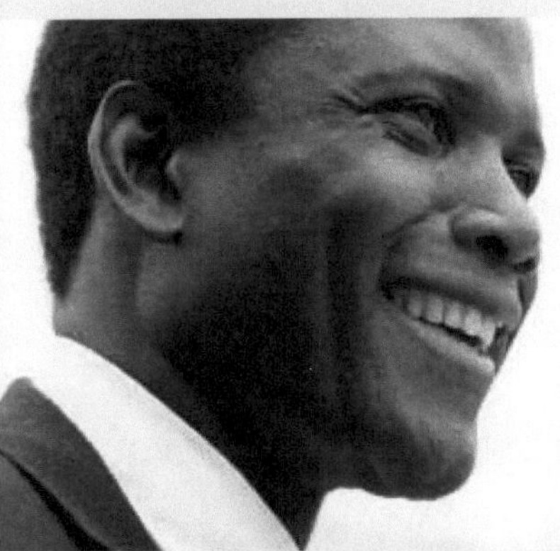

Sidney Poitier was born on February 20, 1927 in Miami, Florida. After a delinquency-filled youth and a short stint in the U.S. Army, he moved to New York to pursue an acting career. He joined the American Negro Theater and later began finding roles in Hollywood. In 1963, he became the first Black actor to win an Academy Award.

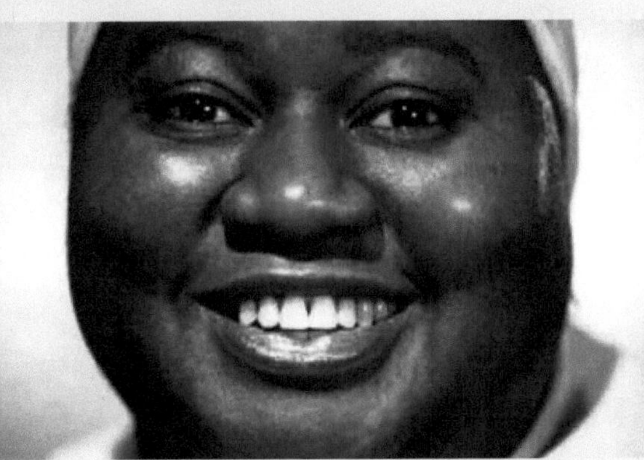

Actress Hattie McDaniel was born June 10, 1895 in Wichita, Kansas. In 1925, she became one of the first African American women on the radio. In 1934, she landed her on-screen break in Judge Priest. She became the first African American to win an Oscar in 1940, for her role as Mammy in Gone with the Wind.

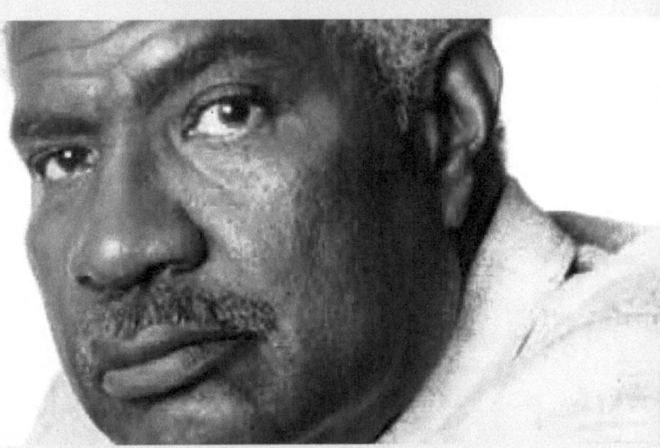

Civil rights activist and actor Ossie Davis was born on December 18, 1917, in Cogdell, Georgia. He attended Howard University in Washington, D.C. Davis met his wife, actress Ruby Dee, and they married in 1948. Over the years, the couple worked on a number of projects together.

I have been deeply concerned for many years by the way African Americans fell through the cracks of history and I reacted by attempting to "set records straight" (through this museum and book.) My attempt was to involve myself with race issues and to write about the remarks and exploits of African Americans.

I share the sentiment of the great Paul Robeson in his words:

> *"We, of this least favored race, realize that our future lies chiefly in our own hands. On ourselves alone will depend the preservation of our liberties and transmission of them, in their integrity to those who will come after us."*

When I first began collecting African American dolls they were plain baby dolls, plain everyday girls and Afro-centric dolls. Just a few of my dolls represented Black women and I think it was because at the time we didn't have a place in history books back in 1976, and few questioned their absence.

One day, I was sitting in my house in Newark, Delaware and I was thinking why not do a section ofBlack women who made a difference in this world and name the dolls after them. My transformation into a historian through researching the achievements of Black women for a section in the doll museum, became rather exciting and a learning tool for me and for my two granddaughters, as well as others. So I decided to do a history of Black women.

I knew the entire process would take several years and in some cases even longer. I knew about the history of Black women, but I have never studied them in-depth.

I then said that it was impossible to display and write a history of Black women, because to my knowledge, there were no

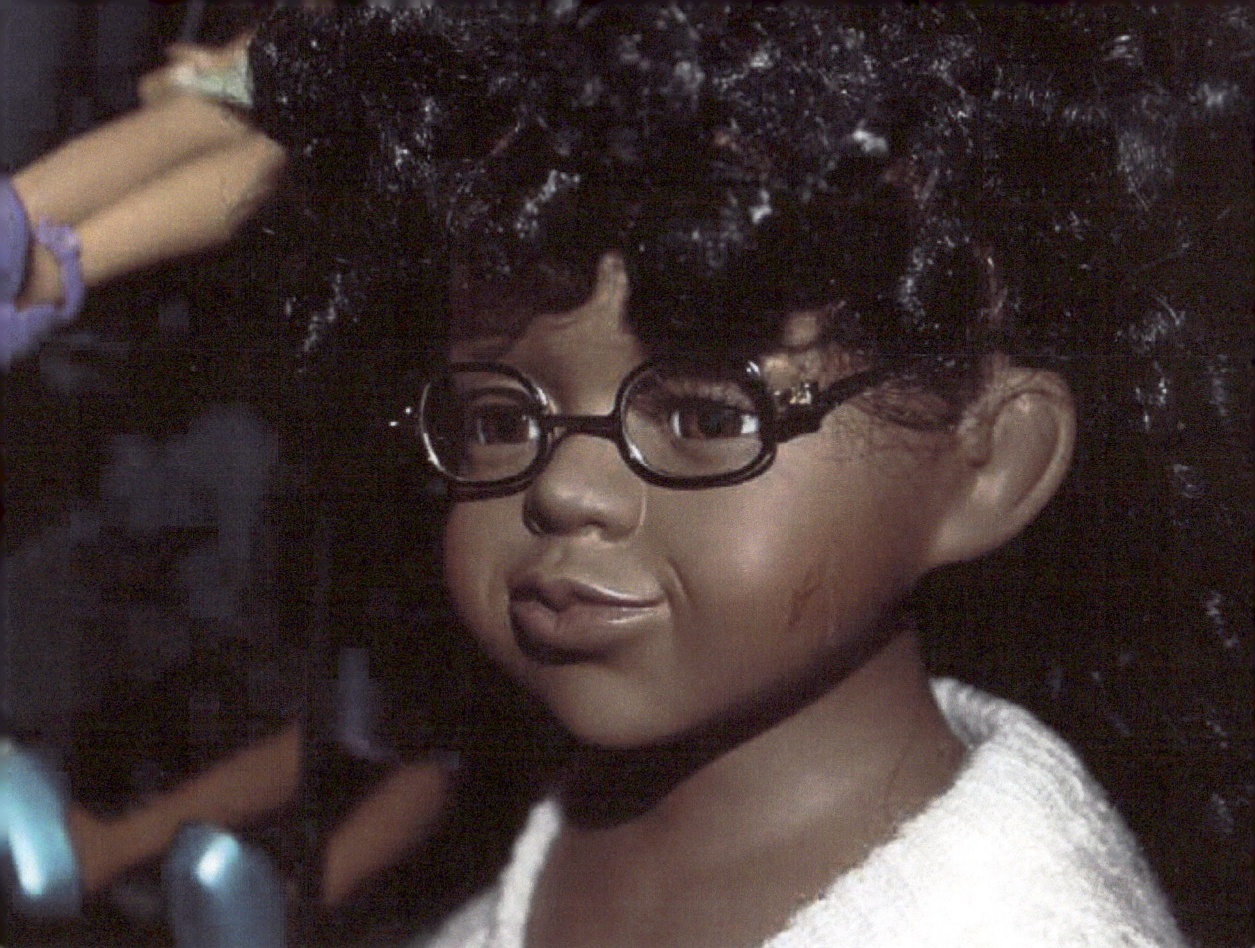

manuscripts, collections or other primary documents and sources in the libraries and archives, but it was going to be exciting to find out about my sisters of color.

Then I said to myself:

> *"Brenda, you are a Black woman. You Love your African American heritage. You mean to tell me that you can't put those two things together and write a history about your doll display of Black women?"*

I have learned in the past twenty years of researching and reading about thousands of Black women from all walks of life—that a special kind of power exists in our history. I hope my books and doll museum will bring others to the self-education and empowerment I have experienced.

A Little About Dolls

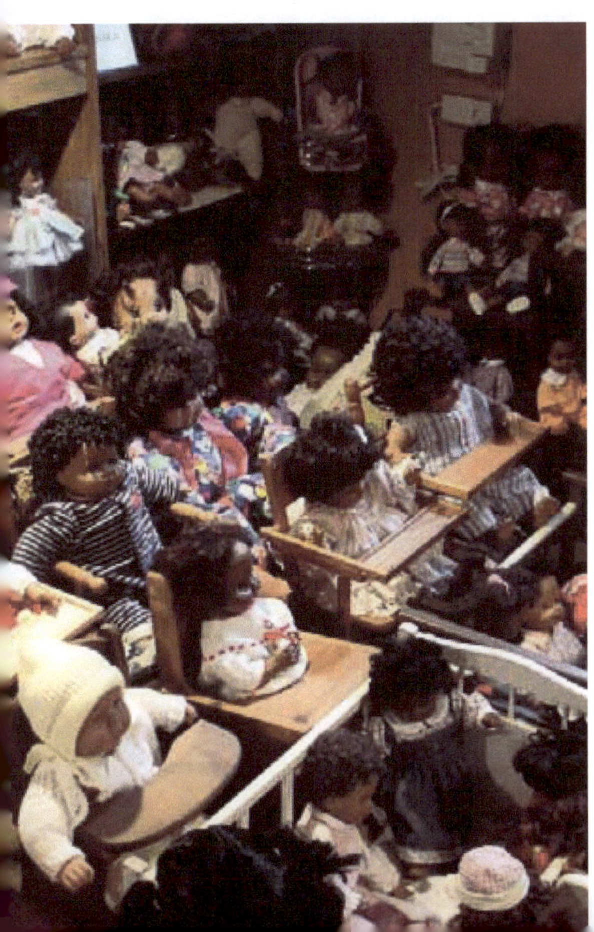

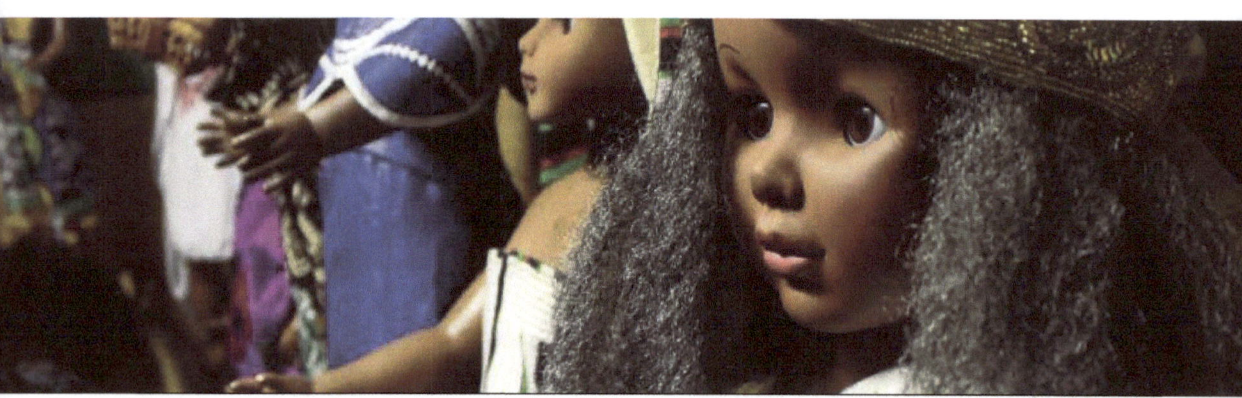

African American dolls are wonderful collectibles. Their historical past unquestionably brings forth an appeal, all on its own. Accordingly, African American dolls date back in the United States and European countries as early as the late 1600s and the early 1800s. From decade-to-decade, Black doll images and popularity have undergone monumental transformations, with each decade bringing about significant changes.

The first African American dolls were made from several materials: cloth, wood, tobacco leaves, kelp, and cornhusks were among the earliest. In the decades between the 1820s and the 1850s, dolls were made from papier mache, a mixture of paper, paste, and water. The makers of these dolls were commonly undocumented.

The papier mache heads were often made and sold separately so that they could later be glued to handmade bodies made of either wood, leather, or dark cloth, with arms and legs made of carved wood. The African American dolls were painted a deep Black, and had exaggerated features and molded kinky hair. Glued on mohair wigs and glass eyes were added later, during the 1850s. The dolls' clothing, hairstyles, and accessories closely imitated those of the slaves and sharecroppers of that period.

Papier Mache Dolls

These dolls were produced primarily in Germany, the United States and Britain. The Leo Moss dolls are among the most notable African American papier mache dolls from this era. Leo Moss was an African American dollmaker who lived in Macon, Georgia, during the late 1800s and the early 1900s.

Leo Moss gained recognition by making portrait papier mache dolls of the African American and Caucasian children in his community. The Moss dolls are extremely rare and command high prices. Accordingly, only 50 currently exist. The papier mache dolls reached their height in popularity in the mid-nineteenth century after the papier mache material was replaced by china.

China Dolls

These dolls had become popular by the mid-nineteenth century. China is a ceramic material with a porcelain glazed finish. Two types of china dolls were produced: the Frozen Charlotte, made of all china, and the china-head doll, which resembled the paper mache dolls.

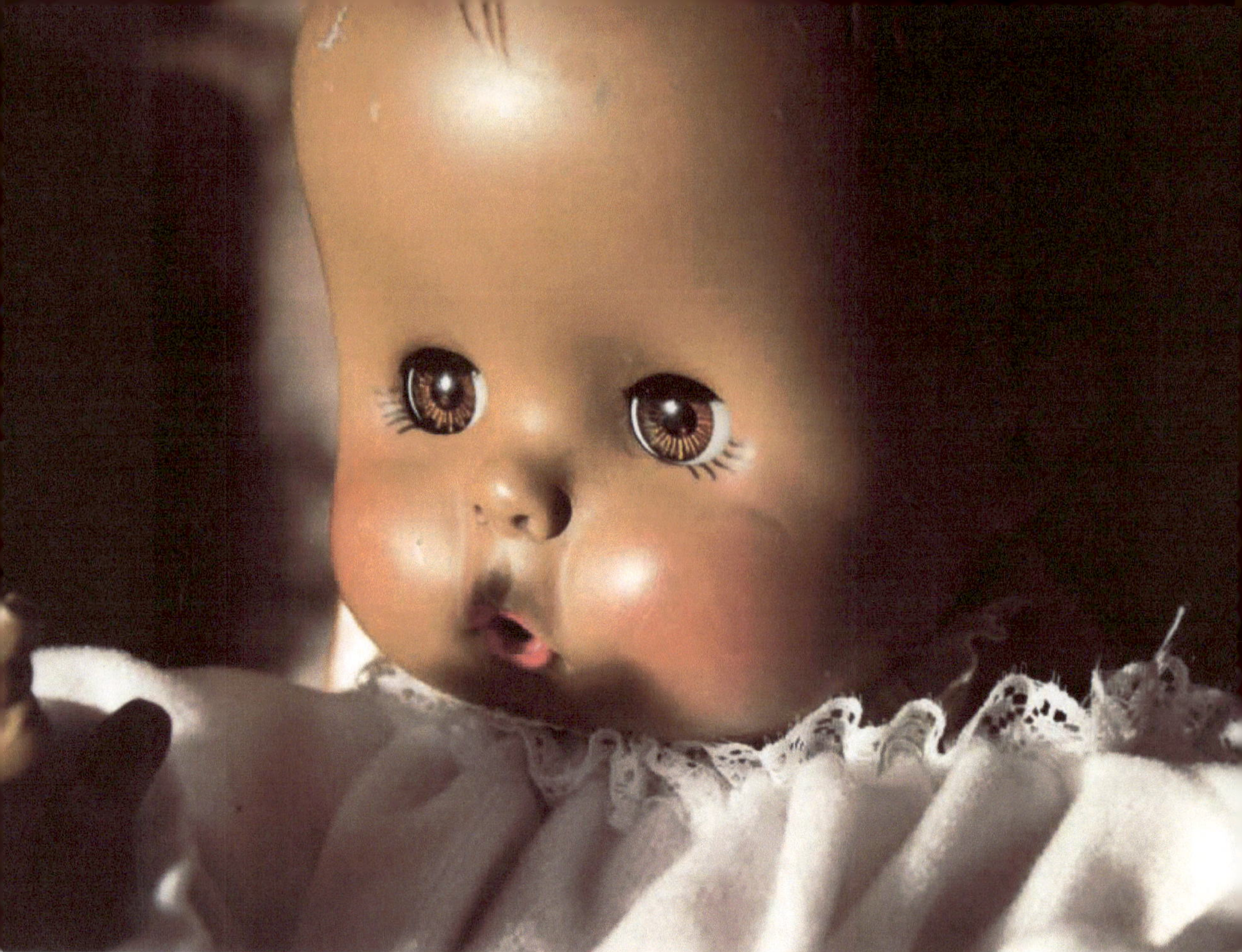

China dolls were manufactured around 1830 and continued to be made well into the 1900s. Their popularity began to decline around 1875. During this time, Bisque was used as the new doll-making material. Bisque is unglazed china.

Bisque Dolls

Accordingly, the bisque dolls brought about the first transformation in African American dolls. With its use, a variety of skin tones were developed, ranging from the darkest shade of black to the lightest shade of brown. The doll's facial and physical features became less exaggerated, and their hairstyles varied.

Their clothing was often made with quality fabric and designed with excellent craftsmanship. Also, it became common practice to use Caucasian molds to produce African American dolls.

African American bisque dolls were produced in very limited quantities, and because most are rare and harder to find, they command higher prices. Germany and France were the primary manufacturers of bisque dolls. Armand Marsellie produced the second-highest number of dolls.

Rag Dolls

Around the early 1900s and through the mid-nineteenth century, the rag doll, the African American Topsy Doll, and the handmade "Mammy Dolls" were prevalent in the United States.

The most famous handmade African American rag doll of this era was Aunt Jemima.

> "African American dolls are wonderful collectibles. Their historical past unquestionably bring forth an appeal all its own."

The Davis Mills Company introduced its first set of Aunt Jemima dolls in 1910. The set was advertised as "Funny Rag Dolls" and was sold as a premium in exchange for four flour coupons and 16 cents. The set included Aunt Jemima; her husband, Uncle Mose; her two children, Diana and Wade Davis.

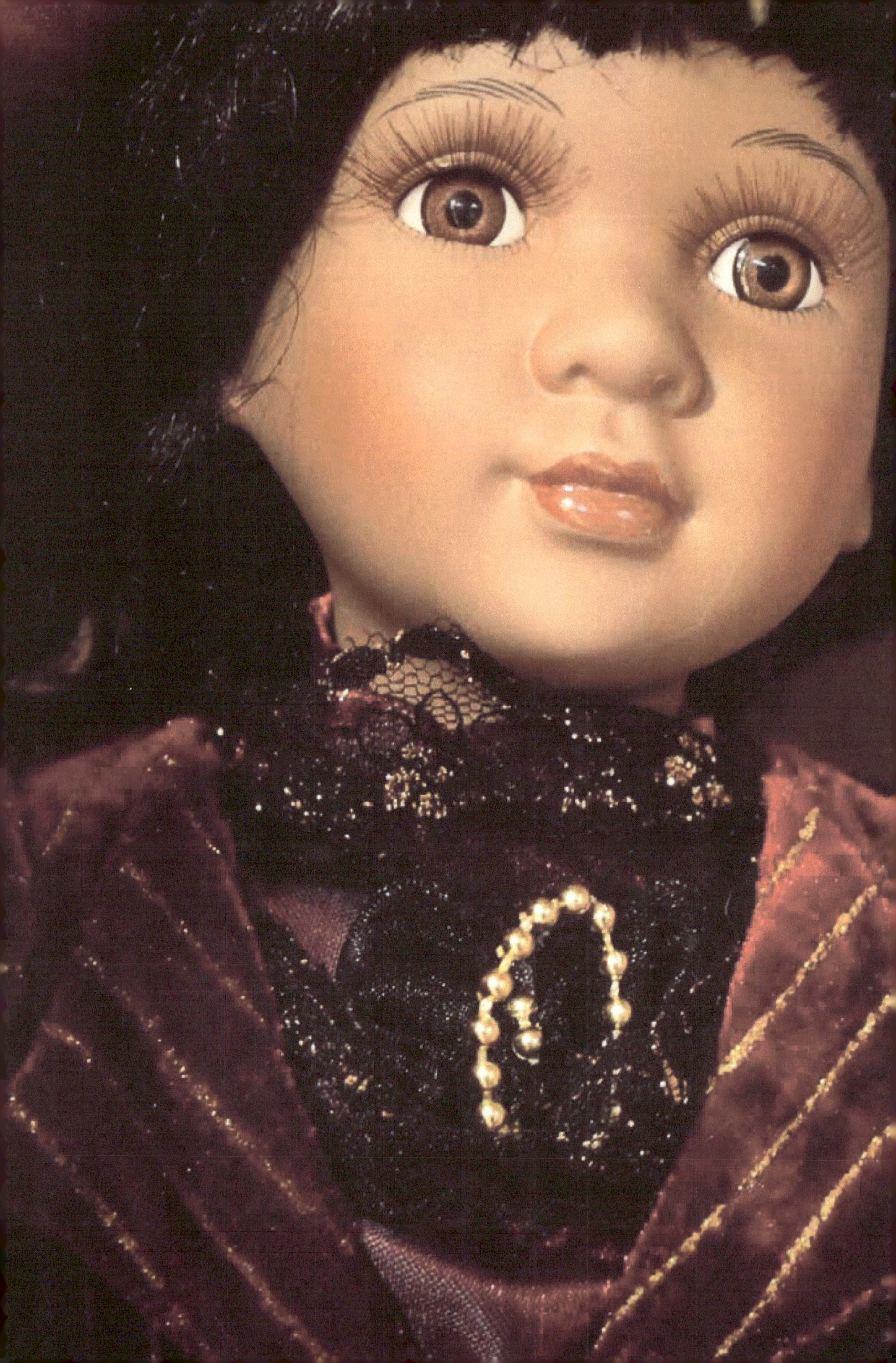

By the late 1920s, the doll industry continued to boom in the European countries and had also become a thriving and prosperous business in the United States.

Composition Dolls

By the 1920s, composition had become the main doll-making material: Madame Alexander, Allied Grand, El Horsman, The Effanbee Doll Company, and the Ideal Novelty and Toy Company were among the top companies producing composition dolls in the United States.

Aunt Jemima was the most popular African American doll manufactured in composition during this period. She was produced using a Caucasian mold and advertised in the Sears Roebuck and Co.'s 1924 catalog in this way:

> *"Little girls delight making believe this Aunt Jemima doll is making delicious pancakes or taking care of their other dolls. Her head is of strong composition finished in pretty chocolate color and she has painted hair, eyes and features."*

By the 1930s, Topsy and Eva composition dolls were popular. Topsy and Eva were both made entirely of composition. Topsy, the African American doll, was dark brown with painted features, and her hair was styled in three pigtails made of thread or mohair. She was often dressed in a one-piece romper. Eva, the Caucasian doll, was usually dressed in an organdy dress with matching bonnet.

Magic Skin (rubber), Hard Plastic and Vinyl Dolls

Magic Skin latex allowed manufacturers to produce dolls with bodies and limbs that resembled the arms and legs of real babies. The three most successful African American latex babies were Amosandra, So-Wee, and Tod-L-Tot, manufactured by the Sun Rubber Company.

The most sought after of the three, was named after the imaginary girl of Amos and Ruby Jones, characters heard over NBC and CBS on the Amos 'n" Andy radio show—Amosandra. She was introduced on Valentines Day in 1949 and sold throughout the 1950s.

So-Wee and Tod-L-Tot followed and were also sold throughout the 1950s. Madam Alexander's first African American doll made of hard plastic was Hilda, produced in 1947, Cynthia, produced in 1952, was her second. Both dolls were created using the Margaret O'Brien face molds. Hilda and Cynthia are both highly collectible and very rare finds. Hilda is particularly rare.

Vinyl was the final material used to make dolls. Discovered during the 1950s, vinyl continues to be the primary material used in the doll industry today. The Ideal Toy Company's Saralee was the most mobilized African American doll produced in vinyl in the 1950s. Life magazine featured Saralee in its May 1951 Issue as "the first anthropologically correct ethnic doll produced for Negro children."

Accordingly, Sara Lee Creech, an insurance saleswoman who worked in interracial groups, and Sheila Burlingame, a sculptress, created Saralee out of Sara Lee Creech's concern for "Negro" children and their relationships with dolls.

The 1950s was the decade that African American dolls began to make their mark on the doll industry. However, the late 1960s marked their new beginnings.

Remco Industries, in 1968, based on the premise that little Negro girls wanted dolls they could identify with more easily and quickly, produced a line of four "ethnically correct Negro dolls". The dolls were Walking Winnie, Growing Sally, Tippy Tumbles, and Baby Grows a Tooth. Remco commissioned Annuel McBurrows, a young African American freelance artist, to design the dolls. The dolls were featured in the toy trade publication Playthings in July 1968. Four Caucasian versions of the dolls were produced using identical names.

Shindana Toy Company is credited as the first and largest manufacturer of African American dolls with African American features. The company grew and prospered as a division of Operation Bootstrap, Incorporated, under the leadership of founders Lou Smith and Robert Hall.

Shindana distributed a line of 32 dolls. Baby Nancy was the first, produced in 1968. Her most distinguished feature was her short, kinky, afro wig. They sold 8,000 Baby Nancy dolls during the 1968 Christmas season.

Beatrice Wright, the Creator, Founder, and President of the first Negro Toy Company to manufacture dolls and stuffed toys, introduced her line of beautifully sculptured African American Dolls. Many believe the Beatrice Wright dolls had more realistic African American features than any of the African American dolls previously attempted.

By the 1970s. African American dolls had become a reputable commodity. The popular dolls of the 1970s were Ideals' "grow hair dolls". Crissy was introduced in 1969.

The succeeding years produced a new generation of African American dolls redesigned for the changing times and evolving lifestyles. In 1985, Yia Eason, an African American businesswoman and the founder of Olmec Toys Incorporated, created a line of African American hairstyling dolls, and Bedtime Kenya.

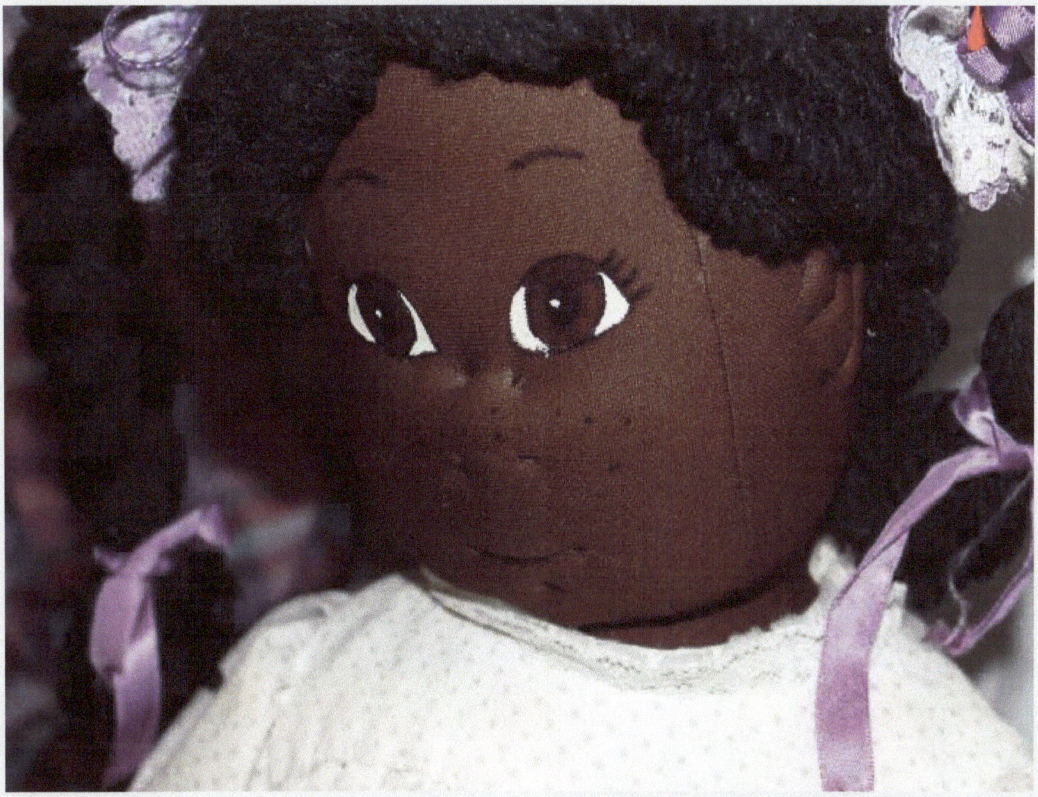

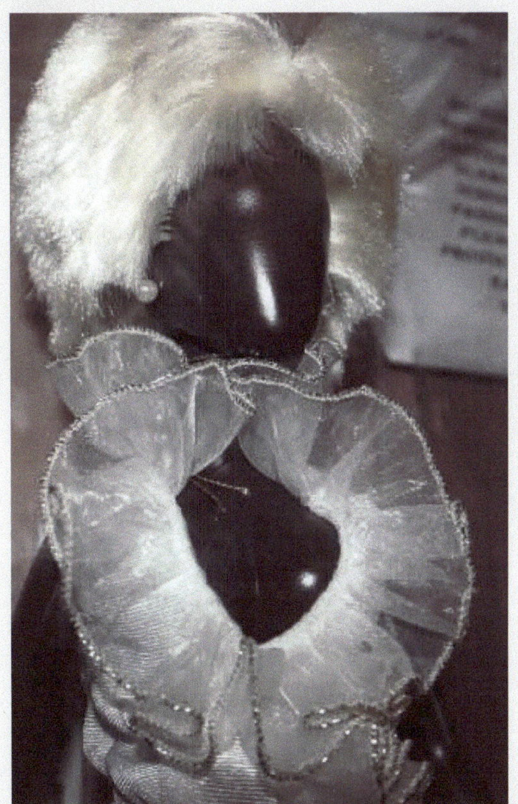

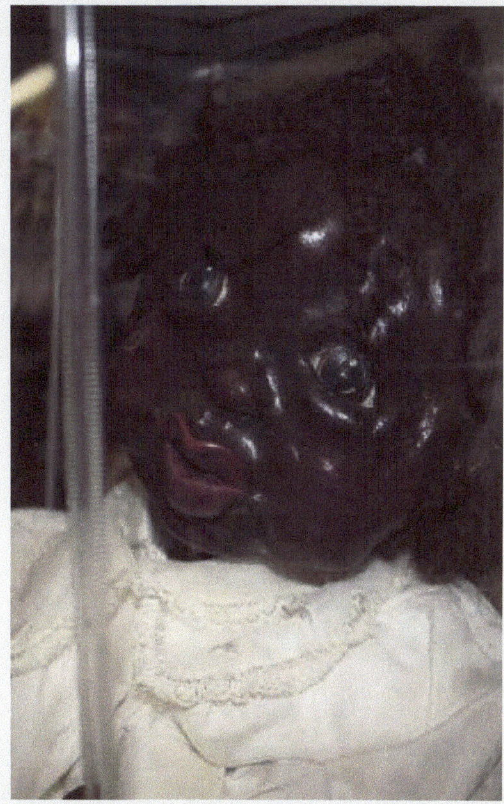

The Black Doll

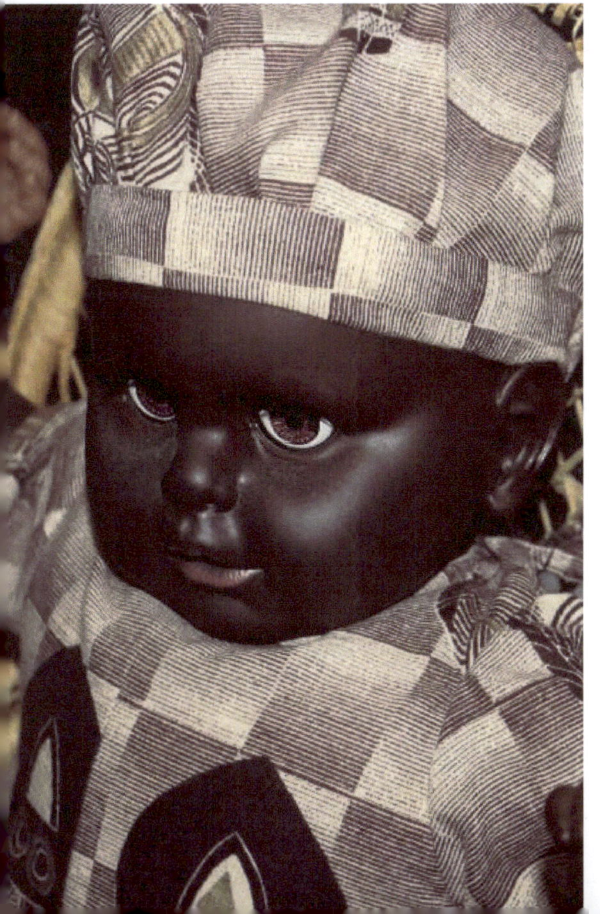

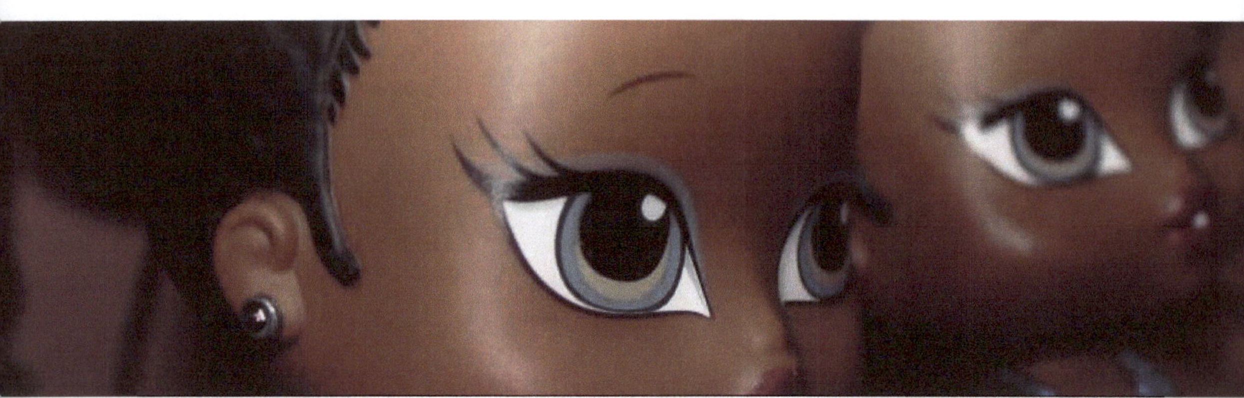

A Black doll is a dark-colored inanimate representation of a dark skinned person. Representations, both stereotyped and accurate fashioned into playthings, date back centuries. More accurate, mass produced depictions are manufactured today as toys and adult collectibles.

Materials used to create Black dolls include bisque, china, cloth, cloth rag dolls composition, hard plastic, paper, papier-mâché, polymer clay, porcelain, silicone resin, vinyl, and wood.

We should note that cloth rag dolls made by American slaves served as playthings for slave children. Early mass produced Black dolls were typically versions of their White counterparts.

During the 1960s and in the aftermath of the Watts Riot in Los Angeles, California, Shindana Toys, a Division of Operation Bookstrap, Inc., is credited as the first major doll company to mass produce ethnically-correct Black dolls, certainly in the United States. Their "dolls made by a dream" with realistic African facial features remain popular amongst Black-doll collectors.

The Mosely African American Doll Collection features different shades of African American skin-toned dolls, organized by category. Some of our categories include: Abolitionist, Africa, Brandi, Birmingham Church Bombing, Biblical women, Baby toddler, Barbie & Ken, Brown-v-Board of Education, Cabbage patch, Civil Rights Era, Crochet dolls, Everyday girls, Glamour girls, Entertainers, Lil Rock Nine, Michel Jackson, NAACP, Olde but Goode, Rag dolls, Ruby Bridges, Scottsboro Boys, Slavery, The Middle Passage and much more.

These dolls reflect my deep belief that to really be proud of whom you are, you have to know and embrace where you come from—"Loving the skin I am in".

Importance of Black Dolls

The importance of Black dolls as playthings for children and collectibles for adults cannot be stressed enough. However, the idea of Black dolls representing the Black population of our society is not new, Black dolls have been available commercially to some extent, often very limited since the second quarter of the nineteenth century. Handmade Black dolls have been a part of African history for centuries.

From the early 1800s to the present, Black dolls, like most other things in our society have gone through many changes. They also experienced great surges in popularity at different times, possibly reflecting attitudes prevalent in our society at a particular given time. In doing research on Black dolls, many questions arise. Some of the most significant ones are as follows:

- Who were the commercial manufacturers of dolls from the early 1800s to the present?
- Where were the dolls made?
- What market were they made for (Black or White children?)
- What materials were used to make the dolls?
- When were their peaks in popularity?
- Most importantly, what do they look like?

These are some of the questions the Mosely Doll Museum will deal with, while examining Black dolls of the past and present. This museum will take you back within the past 75 years through the eyes of children and adults, alike.

I am up every day, thinking and writing about opportunities and ways to make sure that this museum is strong and vibrant to last for the next generation and the one after that, and so on.

As a museum, we will continue to be vigilant in making sure that we are looking after and protecting and mentoring our young girls. We must remember to train up a child in the way she should go. Behind every good man is a good woman, so why not start early.

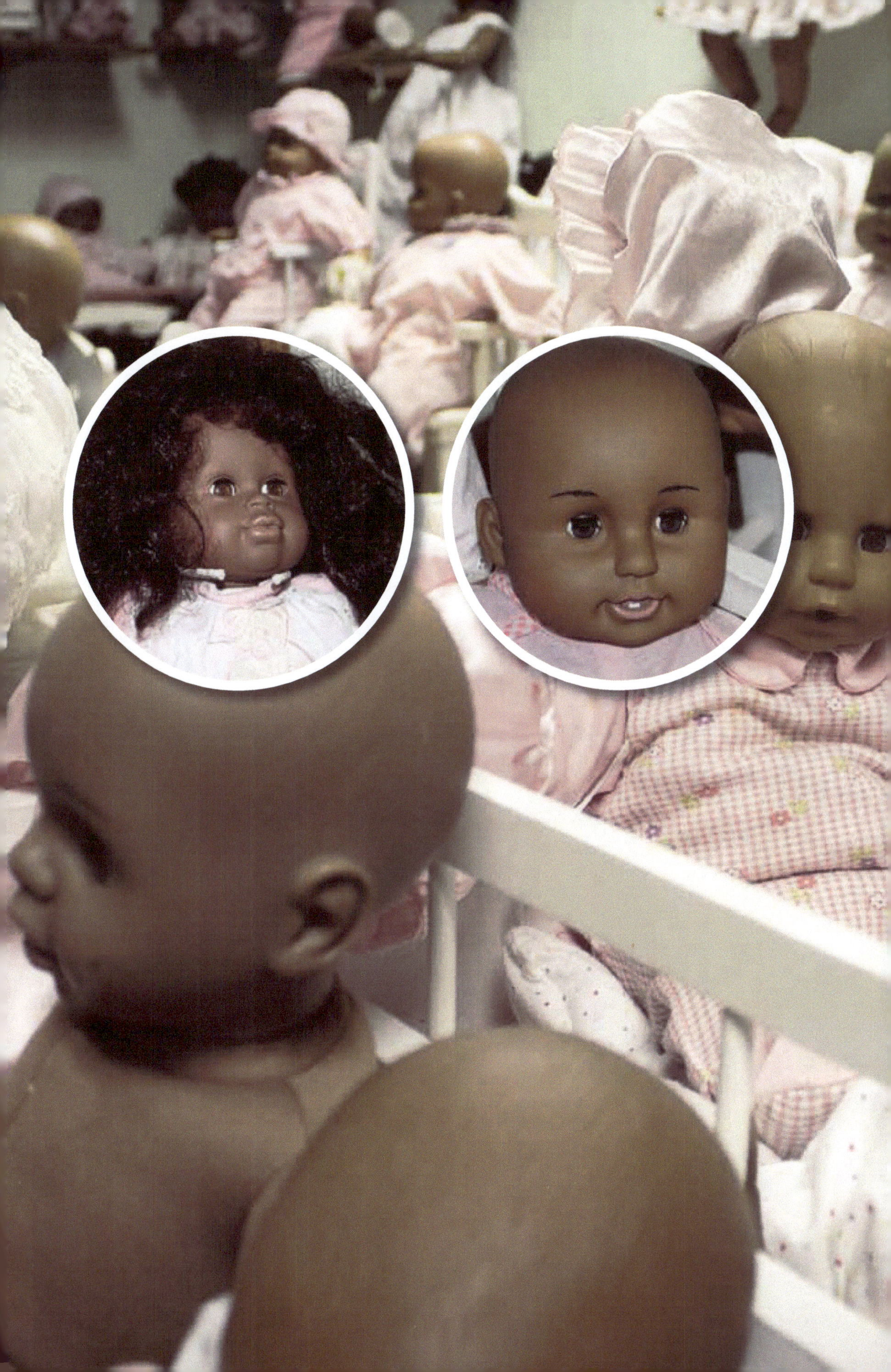

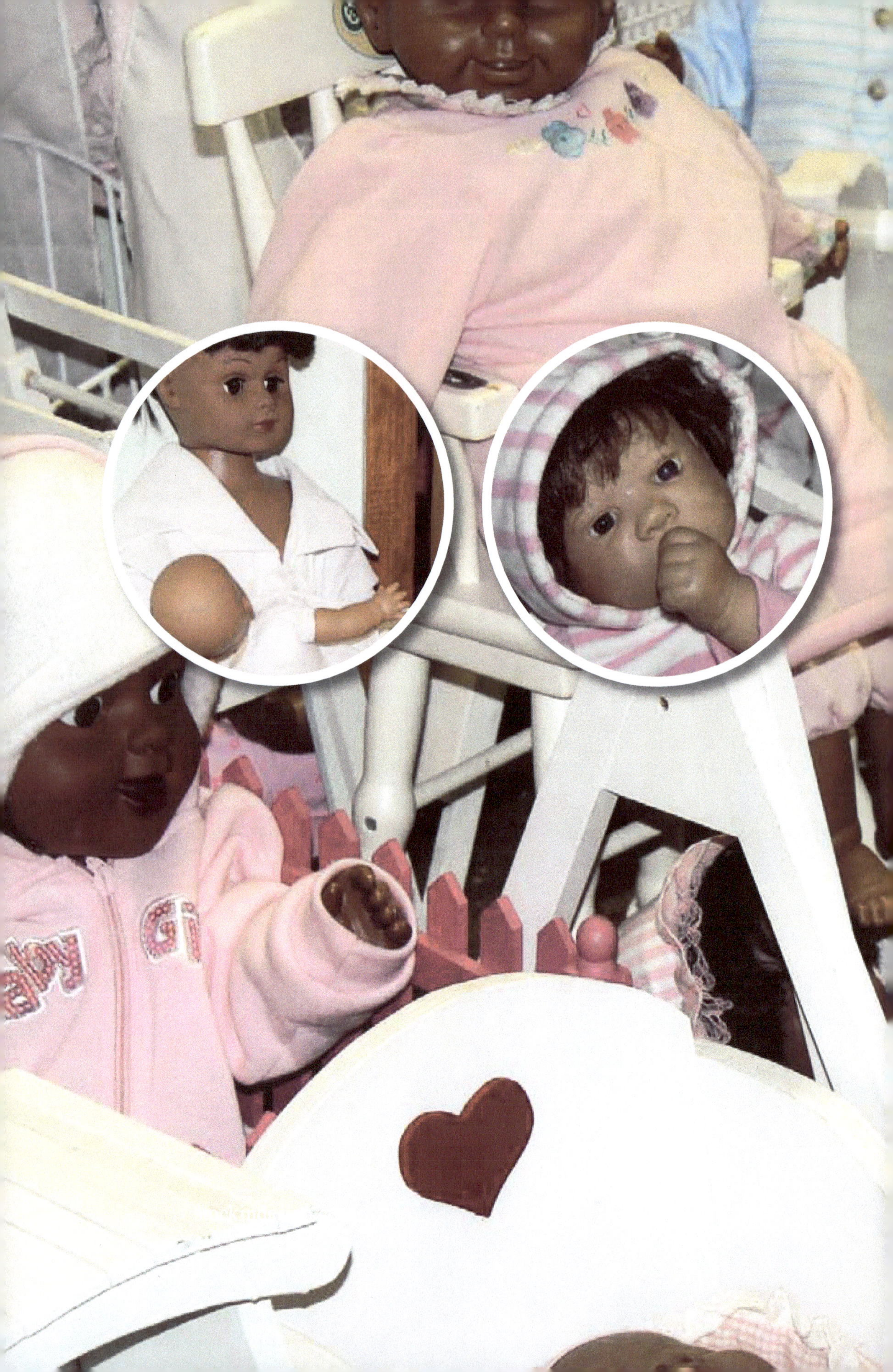

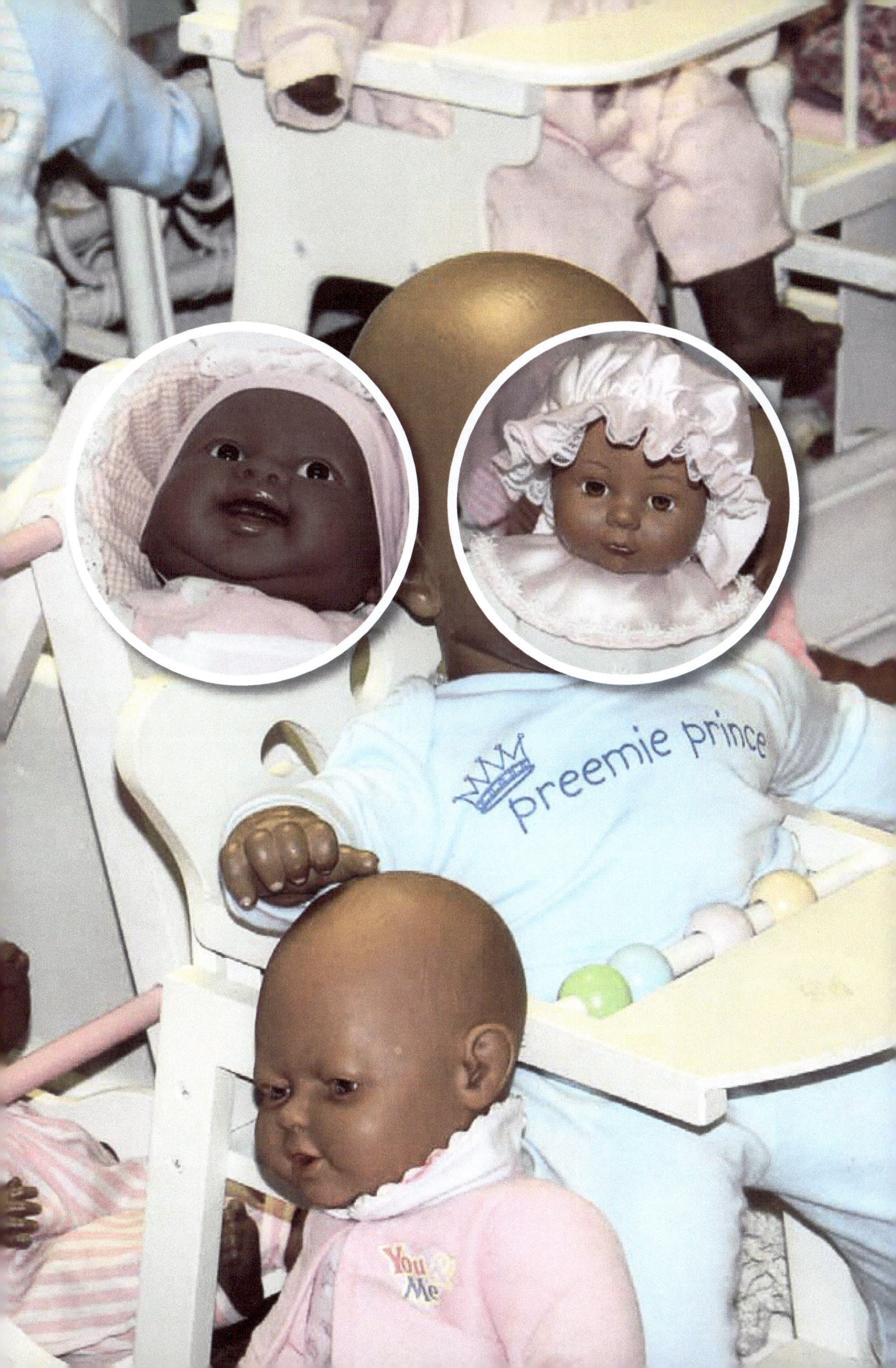
preemie prince
You & Me

The Mission

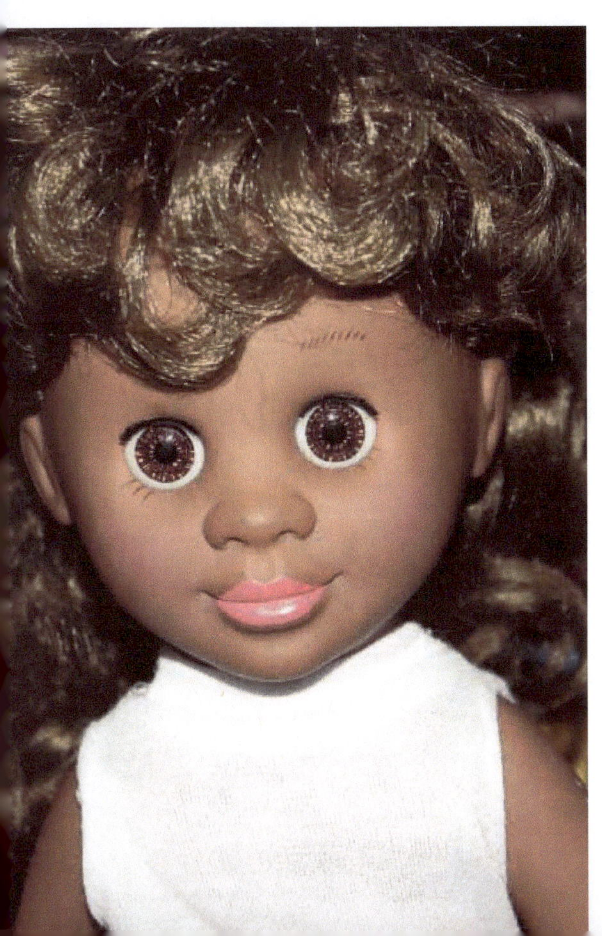

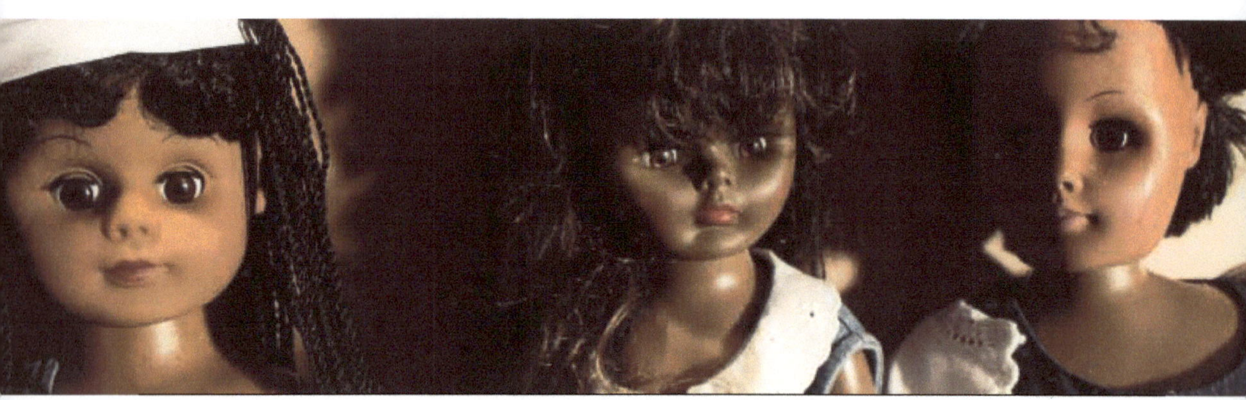

The Mosely African American Doll Collection was established in 1979 as an educational and cultural resource museum dedicated to the research of documented history for the purpose of exhibiting the contributions of Black people from all cultures and geographic locations. Through this museum we strive to promote awareness, knowledge, and understanding among all people while furthering pride, dignity, and inspiration in those who identify directly with this heritage.

To recognize and celebrate African American achievement over the past 100 years, the Mosely African American Doll Collection profiles numerous individuals who have made a lasting and profound impact on our culture. Wherever they've made their mark – arts, business, civil rights, education, entertainment, law, literature, medicine, politics, or sports – the heroes represented in this museum are men, women, and children who have struggled against the odds and advanced to miraculous heights, inspiring countless others in the process. More than 100 exhibits complement this compelling doll collection.

Our mission is:

- To build a museum that would call little girls to go back to playing with dolls, playing house and having tea parties.
- To inspire children to embrace their childhood which they should be enjoying at the ages of 4 to 10.
- To inspire children to embrace their ethnicity and not be ashamed of whom God made them to be.
- To preserve doll history and culture by presenting the art of making and collecting dolls through seminars and lectures; also, to see school buses, and children from all over the Tri-State area taking field trips to see the doll collection in our museum.
- To have group tours and provide transportation to pick up from day cares, youth centers and the orphanages to tour the museum and to participate and attend the workshops.

The Mosely African American Doll Collection is currently located in Newark, Delaware at the home of Eric & Brenda Brown Mosely and has 3,000 plus dolls in its collection. Our prayer is that one day the Lord will bless us with a building that has ample parking space for buses.

We would also like the museum to be located in the city of Wilmington, Delaware. The museum will provide a resource library of information and documentation which highlights the story of how Black people have been perceived through history. The collection includes numerous exhibits/scenes.

Our African American museum collection is based on pride, passion and love. We would be delighted and proud to share the wonderful art, books, decor, dolls, literature, and movies with the public by putting them in a museum for everyone to see.

I have a passion for all the dolls, and all our African American artifacts. They will take you back to when you were a little girl.

There are 3,000 plus Black dolls in the collection that present visual images of how Black people were perceived throughout world history to present day.

> "My mission in life is to put my God-given talents to good use every day; to improve my relationship with God, my family, and my friends, and to give back more than I take."

The Mosely African American Doll Collection is one of a few in the state of Delaware that emphasizes the preservation of Black dolls as artifacts of history and culture.

The majority are from the 1960s to present, however, some of the dolls are between 25 to 50 years old, which includes a delicate early 1900 papier mache one.

As the collection grew and people came to the house, they were amazed and would ask me to make a doll for them—and I was happy to do it. My dream is to create opportunities and better lives for the children of African descent.

The museum is about how to teach children to realize their potential by instilling in them the belief that through discipline, hard work, and self-respect they can attain their highest goals.

Self-esteem, particularly for young African American girls and boys, is the most essential ingredient for success, because all of the old-fashioned values—things like discipline, respect, integrity, and courage are given life.

Discipline and learning to establish a goal and remain focused until it's accomplished, regardless of the distractions. Poverty is not an excuse for laziness, nor is anger.

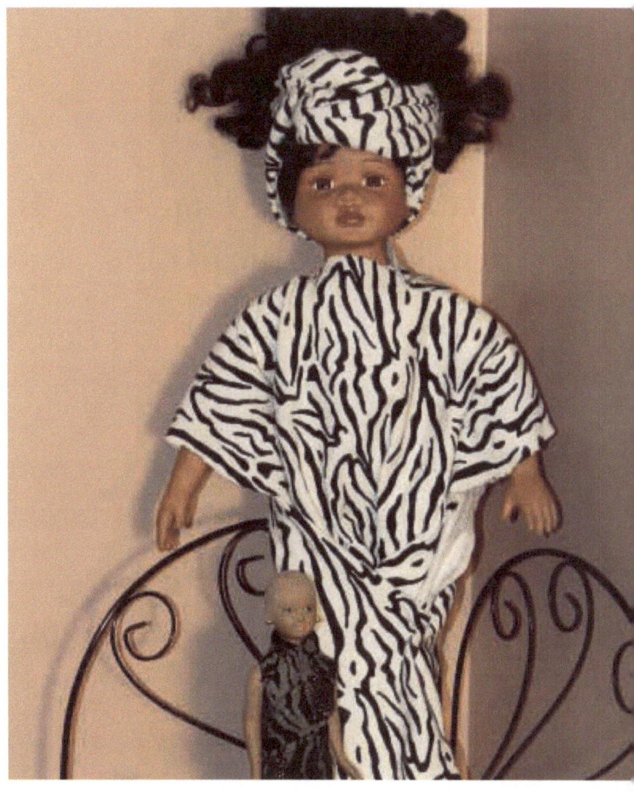

The "currency" here is the sense of security, the sense of belonging to something, the sense that we are not going to abandon the children because they had a difficult time adjusting to a particular situation.

The relationship between children and adults is based on kinship, not indebtedness.

My Personal Mission Statement:

My mission in life is to put my God-given talents to good use every day; to improve my relationship with God, my family, and my friends, and to give back more than I take.

Prayer

Total dependence on GOD. The LORD is my shepherd and I'm thrilled to belong to Him.

For it is thus that I shall flourish and thrive no matter what life may bring to me. Psalms 23:

> *"The LORD is my shepherd; I shall not want. He maketh me lie down in green pastures: he leadeth me beside still waters."*
>
> *"He restoreth my soul; he leadeth me in the paths of righteousness for his name sake. Yea, though I walk through the valley of the shadow of death, I will fear no evil: for thou art with me: thy rod and thy staff, they comfort me."*
>
> *"Thou preparest a table before me in the presence of mine enemies; thou anointest my head with oil; my cup runneth over. Surely goodness and mercy shall follow me all the days of my life: and I will dwell in the house of the LORD forever."*

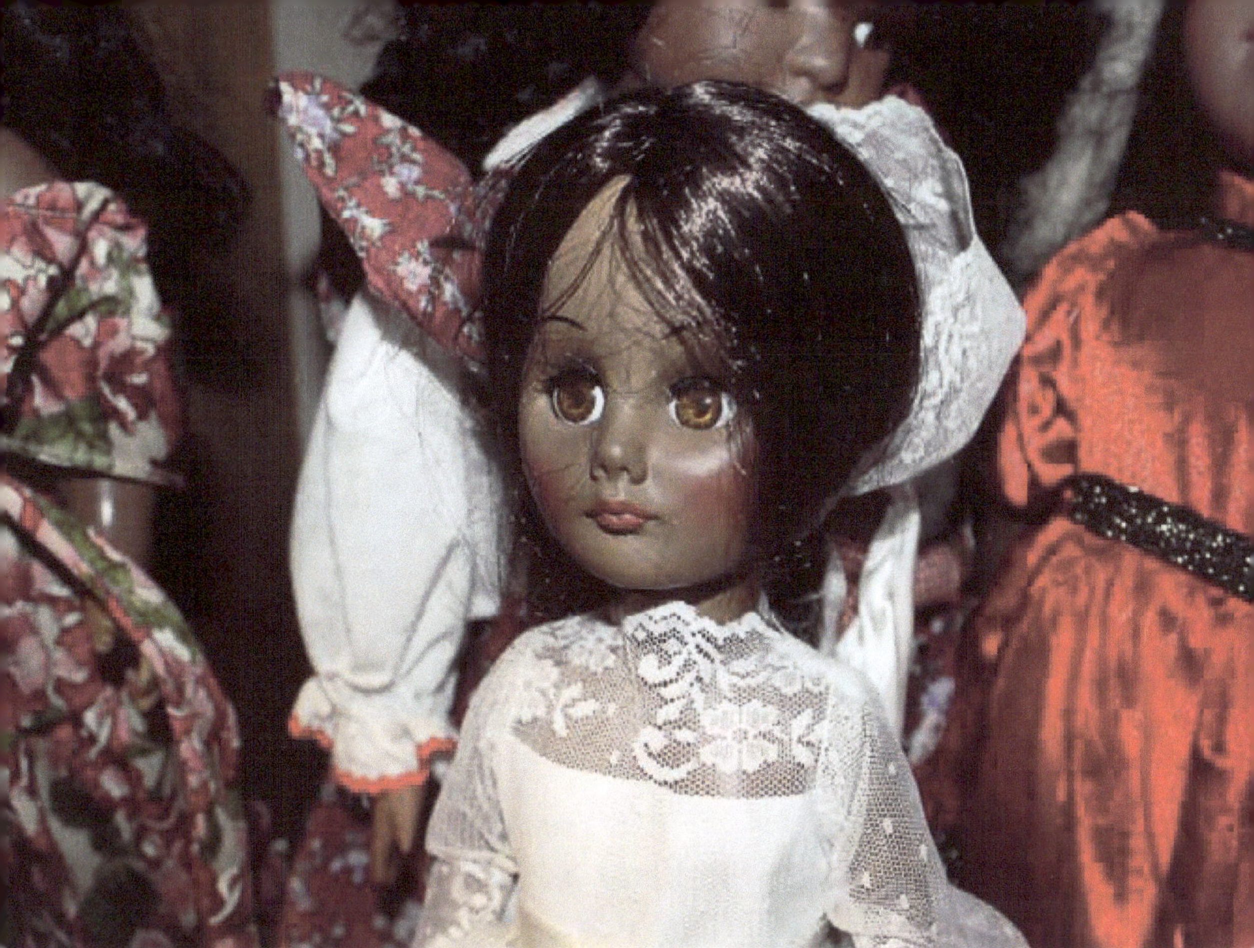

Praise and Gratitude

There is nobody GREATER than the LORD, total dependence on GOD.

Guidance

GOD is the only one who knows my past, present and future; my capabilities and needs. He alone can open and close all doors so my prayer should be:

> *Teach me thy way, O LORD, and lead me in a plain path.— Psalms 27:11*

> *Trust in the LORD with ALL thine heart; and lean not unto thine own understanding. In ALL THY WAYS acknowledge him, and HE SHALL DIRECT THY PATHS.— Proverbs 3: 5, 6*

Growth

Increase and mature physically, mentally, and spiritually—Genesis 21:26 Luke 2:40.

> *Be careful for nothing; but in everything by prayer and supplication with thanksgiving let your request be made known unto God.— Philippians 4:6*

Confidence

> *The LORD is my light and my salvation; who shall I fear. The LORD is the strength of my life; of whom shall I be afraid? — Psalm 27:3,4*

> *The LORD shall be thy confidence, and shall keep thy foot from being taken.— Proverbs 3:26.*

> *And let us not be weary in well doing; for in due season we shall reap if we faint not.— Galatians 6:9*

Discipline

Includes training and knowledge balanced with correction and punishment; based in love and concern for my well-being, its purpose is our maturity and happiness.—Psalm 94:12-13, Proverbs 3:11-12

Discouragement

Can be caused by circumstances beyond a person's control: dead-end job, criticism from friends and family, etc. It can also arise from a sense of failure or inadequacy, which could be caused even by seemingly insignificant factors in a person's life.

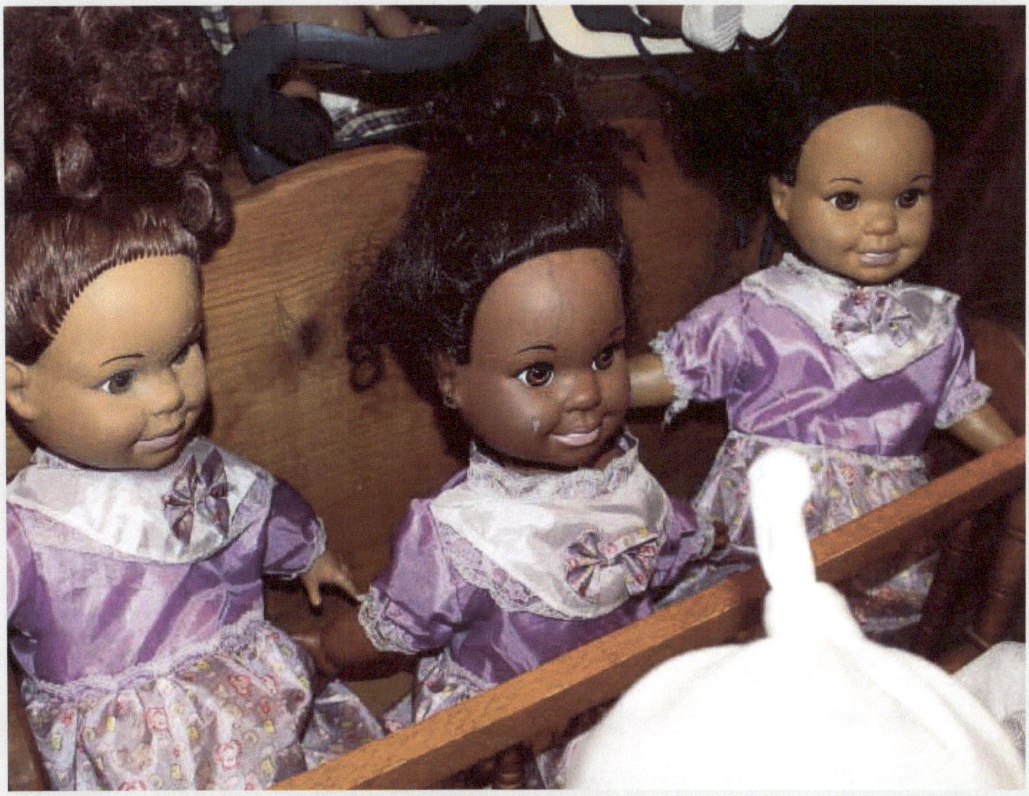

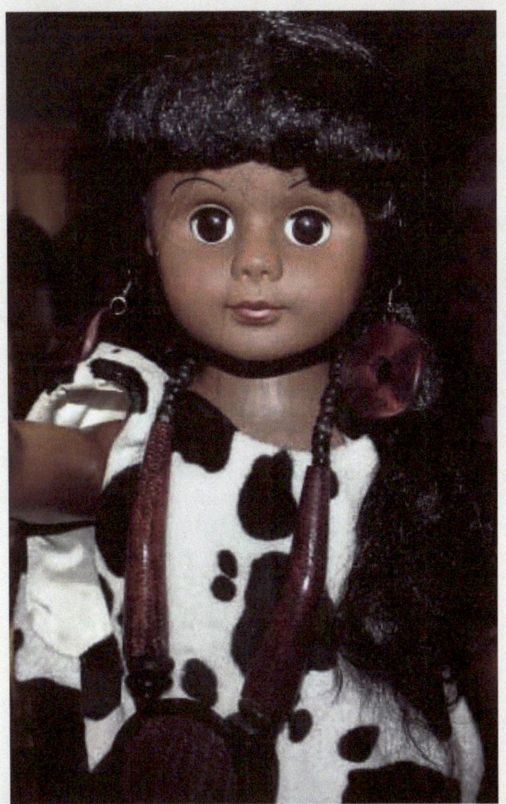

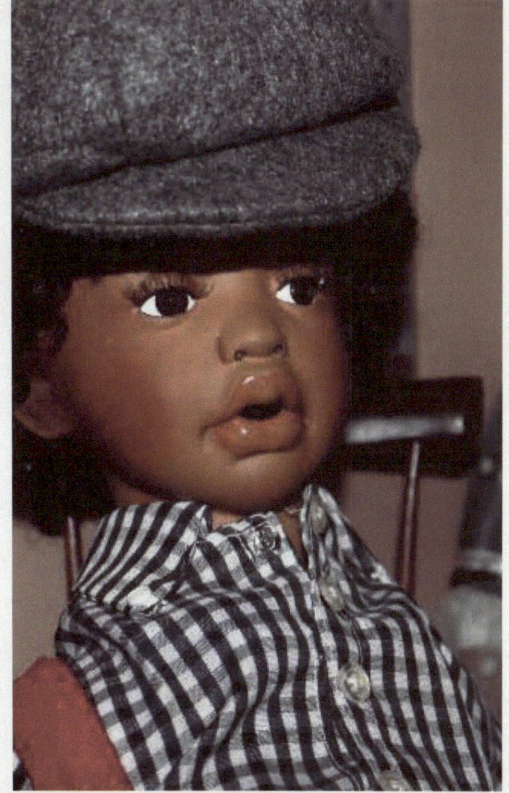

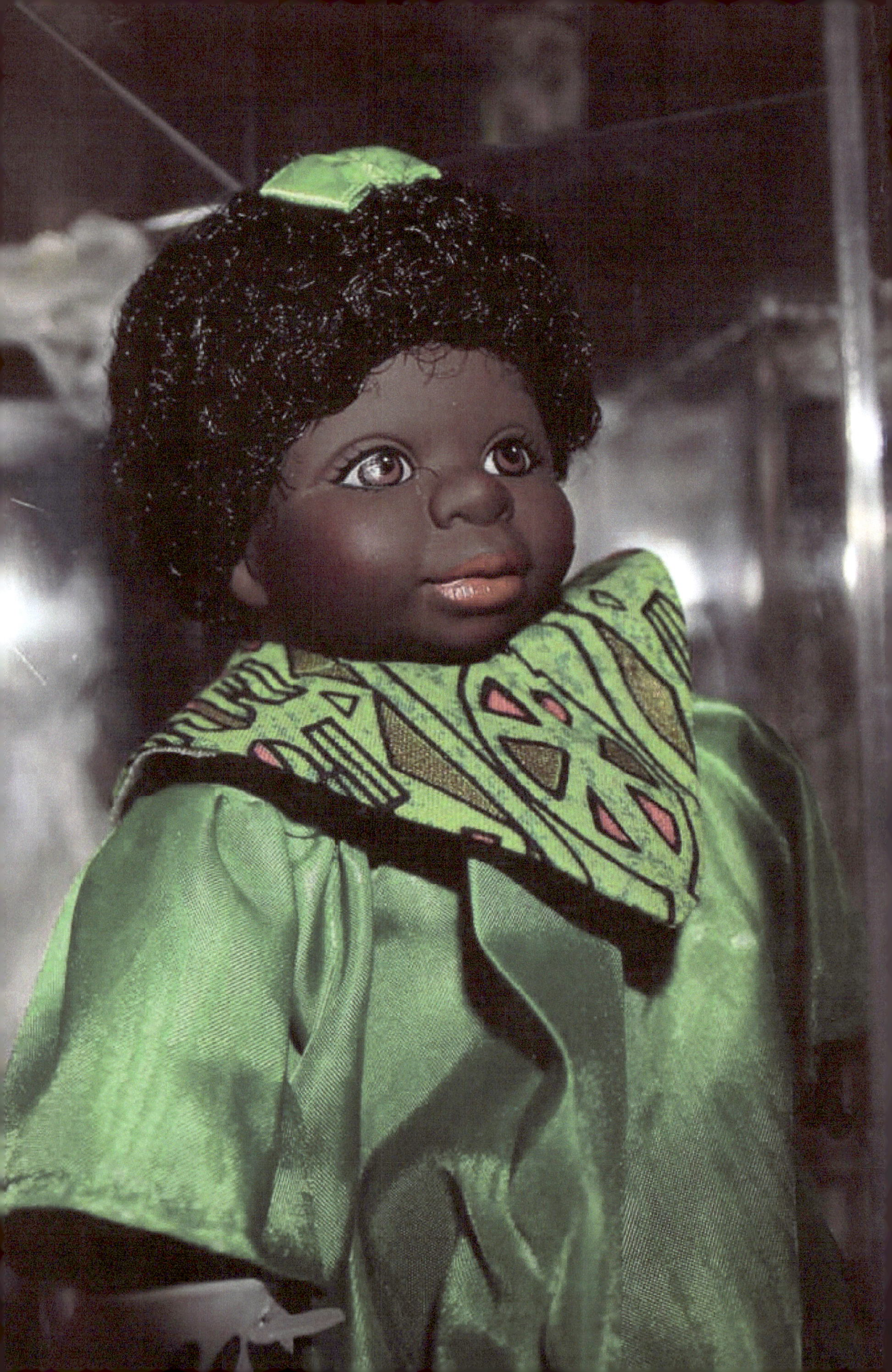

These factors can gradually multiply into a grave problem with self-esteem.

> *No matter what happens, always be thankful, for this is God's will for you who belong to Christ Jesus.— 1 Thessalonians 5:18*

> *Because the Lord God helps me, I will not be dismayed; therefore I have set my face like flint to do his will and I know that I will triumph. — Isaiah 52:7*

Pride and Ego

Do not have a strong ego and pride that it gets in the way of a proper relationship with God and others. The opposite of pride is humility, which involves being realistic about one's vulnerability and looking upon oneself as a servant of others.

A humble person does not feel or act superior and does not show favoritism in his dealings with others.

> *Pride ends in destruction; humility ends in honor.— Proverbs 18:12*

Strength

The state, quality or property of being strong; physical power. I Can!

> *I can do all things through Christ which strengthens me.— Philippians 4:13*

Giving and Tithing

We are to give freely of that which we have received; we are responsible for the right use of all our gifts. To give means to be committed to the stewardship of one's possessions for God. To tithe is to present a tenth of our prosperity to God: whether money, objects of value, or talents and time.

> *For if you give, you will get! Your gift will return to you in full and overflowing measure, pressed down, shaken together to make room for more, and running over. Whatever measure you use to give large or small will be used to measure what is given back to you.— Luke 6:38*

Wisdom

Understanding knowledge gained by experience.— 2 Chronicles 9:23 1 Corinthians 1:17

www.ingramcontent.com/pod-product-compliance
Lightning Source LLC
LaVergne TN
LVHW070509120826
845147LV00031BA/268
* 9 7 8 0 6 1 5 7 6 0 6 8 1 *